THE NEW CATHOLIC TREASURY
OF WIT AND HUMOR

The New Catholic Treasury of Wit and Humor

Edited by PAUL BUSSARD

and the Editors of the *Catholic Digest*

Illustrated by Charles Geer

MEREDITH PRESS / NEW YORK

Library of Congress Catalog Card Number: 68-12134
Manufactured in the United States of America for Meredith Press

Preface

Eight years ago the first *Catholic Treasury of Wit and Humor* made its appearance. Much to the delight of the *Catholic Digest* editors who had worked hard and long to put it together, it was a success. In view of the subject matter we probably should say "howling success," but we shall refrain from that extravagance.

Here we are again with a second collection of amusing articles and droll sayings culled from the pages of our magazine. Readers will discover that many of the chapters contain articles about Pope John XXIII. We think the reason is obvious: Pope John himself loved laughter, and his writings and conversations were filled with delightful flashes of wit. If anyone deserves to be quoted or written about in a collection of humor, it is surely the warmhearted, genial Good Pope John.

We hope the *New Catholic Treasury of Wit and Humor* brings happy moments to all who read it.

Paul Bussard

Acknowledgments

The editors and publisher wish to thank all those individuals whose names are appended to their contributions and to acknowledge with gratitude the additional cooperation of the following or their representatives:

Marjorie Earl for "The Day I Met Pope John" from the *Star Weekly Magazine*, copyright © 1959 by the Toronto Star, Ltd.

G. K. Chesterton for "The Roots of the World" from *Lunacy and Letters*, copyright © 1958 by Dorothy Collins and published by Sheed & Ward.

Phyllis McGinley for "The Wit of Saints" from *Vogue*, copyright © 1962 by Condé Nast Publications and reprinted with permission of Curtis Brown, Ltd.

Sister Mary Corde Lorang for "Five Nuns at a Bullfight" from *Footloose Scientist in Mayan America*, copyright © 1966 by the Maryknoll Sisters of St. Dominic, Inc., and reprinted by permission of Charles Scribner's Sons.

Elwood D. Baumann for "Oodles of Noodles in Hong Kong" from *Catholic Digest*, copyright © 1961 by The Catholic Digest, Inc.

A. R. McElwain for "A Chat with Ronald Knox" from *Catholic Digest*, copyright © 1960 by The Catholic Digest, Inc.

Bernard Basset, S.J., for "Eight Nuns in an Austin" from *Priest in the Piazza*, copyright © 1963 by Bernard Basset, S.J., and reprinted by permission of the Academy Guild Press.

Bernard Godwin for "Portrait of a Pope" from *America*, copyright © 1959 by America Press.

Acknowledgments

Theodore Irwin for "The Wistful World of Brother Juniper" from *Coronet,* copyright © 1960 by Esquire, Inc.

Harold Helfer for "Little Moe" from *Catholic Digest,* copyright © 1963 by The Catholic Digest, Inc.

Mary Dana Rodriguez for "O'Malley and the Little Nuns" from *Catholic Digest,* copyright © 1961 by The Catholic Digest, Inc.

Edwin Newman for "Mr. Spooner and Mrs. Malaprop" from *TV Guide,* copyright © 1963 by Triangle Publications, Inc.

R. J. Heathorn for "Learn with Book" from *Punch,* copyright © 1962 by Punch.

Frank Scully for "I Built a Chapel" from *View,* copyright © 1961.

Harold Dunn for "Kids Have the Answers" from *Catholic Digest,* copyright © 1964 by The Catholic Digest, Inc.

Barrett McGurn for "Pope John XXIII" from *Catholic Digest,* copyright © 1959 by the Catholic Digest, Inc.

Dal Stivens for "Animals Have Their Fun" from the *Rotarian,* copyright © 1964 by Rotary International.

H. Allen Smith for "Kids Write What They Think" from *Don't Get Perconal with a Chicken,* copyright © 1957, 1959 by H. Allen Smith and reprinted by permission of Little, Brown & Co.

Phyllis McGinley for "Women Are Better Drivers" from the *American Weekly,* copyright © 1959 by Hearst Publishing Co., Inc., and reprinted by permission of Curtis Brown, Ltd.

Jean Kerr for "The Ten Worst Things About a Man" from *McCall's,* copyright © 1959 by McCall Corp.

Parke Cummings for "Women Want to Know Everything" from the *Rotarian,* copyright © 1961 by Rotary International.

Francis Sugrue for "Pope John Today" from *Popes in the Modern World,* copyright © 1961 by Francis Sugrue and reprinted with permission of Thomas Y. Crowell Co.

Phyllis McGinley for "Laughter in Our Family" from *The Province of the Heart,* copyright © 1958, 1959 by Phyllis McGinley and published by Viking Press.

John E. Gibson for "Women Are Funny" from *Catholic Digest,* copyright © 1963 by The Catholic Digest, Inc.

John J. Ryan for "Two-Car Family" from *Columbia,* copyright © 1963 by the Knights of Columbus.

Contents

Contents

IV. IN OUR PARISH

V. SMALL FRY

VI. THE GOOD SHEPHERD AND THE ANIMAL FLOCK

VII. THE THOUGHTS OF YOUTH

VIII. EXAMINATION AND CONFESSION

IX. FAMILY CIRCLE

X. THIS HEALTHY LIFE

XI. NO CITY OF GOD

I THE GREAT AND THE NEAR GREAT

Illustration from *The Wit of Saints*

The Day I Met Pope John

ॐ

BY MARJORIE EARL

Last summer [1959] I met Pope John. While time may dissolve the details of that meeting, I know I'll never forget the sudden surge of relaxation and pleasure I felt when I stood before him.

A meeting with the leader of the world's 496 million Catholics and 263rd vicar of Christ on earth might be expected to ruffle a more disciplined composure than mine. That it didn't is due to the fact that this serene man of seventy-eight carries tranquillity about with him like a blanket to warm every chill of self-consciousness that a visitor may have.

Tranquillity accompanies him into a room. It rests visibly on his broad, smooth forehead. It is drawn into the deep laugh wrinkles that circle his face like rings around the moon. It beams out through gray-green eyes as alert as soldiers on parade.

"He has always been serene," says his niece, Enrica Roncalli. She used to keep house for him when, as Cardinal Archbishop of

3

Venice, he spent his holidays in the northern Italian village of his birth, Sotto il Monte.

"He always loved to have visitors, too," she adds. That explains in part why meeting him was like visiting a dear old uncle who had suddenly and unexpectedly come up in the world.

The visitor's sense of relaxation when he finally meets the Pope has permeated the Vatican. Everyone has felt the warmth of his presence, from cardinals, whose number he increased to an unprecedented seventy-five, to carpenters, whose work he once interrupted to share a bottle of wine with them.

Until I actually felt the impact of the Pope's personality, I missed the significance of the cheerful smiles and the expansive gestures that directed me through the great bronze door to my high moment in the apostolic palace. An elevator took me to the papal apartments. I was in a nervous sweat.

I felt as rattled as the elevator operator was recently. He found himself, for the first time in history, with the Holy Father as a passenger. Pope John has a private elevator, but that morning he sailed unannounced into the public one. The operator stood frozen at attention until his passenger tapped him gently on the shoulder. "Unless you do something, my son, we may be here all day."

"Where do you wish to go, Holy Father?" asked the operator.

"Down," replied the Pope, off on another unscheduled inspection of his domain.

I was shown into a splendid rectangle of a room decorated with fifteenth-century frescoes and tapestries. It was dominated at one end by a huge red-and-gold throne on a carpeted dais.

Pope John is said to be considering the abolition of much of the pomp that surrounds the papacy. When he was crowned in November [1958], he asked that the exotic, traditional ceremony be modified, if it could not be entirely eliminated.

4

"The Pope is no longer a temporal prince," he said. "He is a priest, a father, and a shepherd. He has no need of exterior pomp."

I was grateful for the diversion of exterior pomp. I arrived a cautious half hour or more before I was summoned to the final lap of my progress into the Pope's presence.

I sat nervously on the edge of one of the uncomfortable chairs that line the walls. I found myself in an anxious company of monks, priests, nuns, men in sober suits, and women. Only a few of the women wore the long, black dresses and the veils that used to be mandatory. I had asked about a long dress and was told I didn't even have to wear black. Something dark and modest would be suitable.

Semiprivate audiences, which may include any number from six to forty, take place in a series of brightly ornamented rooms through which the Pope moves like a shaft of sunlight. About thirty-five were at the one I attended. Most of them, like me, had arrived in a state of great anxiety. A chamberlain and a resplendent guardsman moved about soothing us with small talk.

For all his relaxation, Pope John is a stickler for courtesy. His guests must be made to feel at home, particularly if he is not quite ready to receive them. And he usually isn't. Pope John, I was told, usually ignores the time. That turns nearly every ceremony upside down.

We were all present and accounted for long before he showed up. He might have popped in on us while nobody was looking had not his arrival been heralded by a noticeable increase of tension. We stiffened to attention as a guard stretched his neck to look out the door. The chamberlain seemed to be counting heads while he removed a couple of flushed latecomers from the exit.

A pair of newlyweds from Leeds exchanged deep looks and decided to hold hands. Three Canadian nuns from Rimouski stared rigidly across the room at five Italian nuns from Brescia, who betrayed their anxiety by the tremor of the white organdy bows standing stiffly at their throats.

An American woman leaned over me to hiss to her friend, "Did you remember to bring the rosaries?" Wordlessly the friend unzipped a shopping bag to disclose a tangle of gilt and beads. Just then the sound of applause, followed by laughter, drifted in from the next room. That ended the whispers.

We turned our eyes toward the entrance. It was a theatrical moment, but Pope John, who is not a theatrical man, threw it away.

He came in like a gust of wind, his step light and confident in his red velvet shoes. He is quite as jolly looking as I expected him to be from his photographs, although somewhat smaller in stature.

He has big ears, a big nose, and big, gentle hands. A fuzz of white hair surrounds his white zucchetto (skullcap). His pectoral cross rests firmly on his broad chest. His white cassock hangs at a radical angle over his stout figure and droops at the back because he habitually thrusts his hands into his pockets when he talks.

He looks for all the world as though he had just stepped down from the frame of a Renaissance painting, with his total aspect of serene benevolence fixed forever by an artist who had worked long and lovingly over every detail.

His first act was to smile to us all until his entire face seemed involved in an outpouring of affection. Unfortunately the first radiance was lost on most of us, for we sank in unison to our knees. We might have remained there indefinitely if the chamberlain had not scampered about urging us to get up. In reverence for his office, princes and peasants alike kneel before the Pope and kiss the fisherman's ring on the third finger of his right hand. But more than this he would like to avoid.

6

Behind the hearty little man so ready with a funny anecdote —who can joke to a kneeling guardsman, "Get up. After all, you're a captain and I was only a sergeant"; who can say to a nervous young pastor, "Don't worry, I'm a new boy, too"—is a man of religion, "humble as dust and ashes." His eyes proclaim that he is constantly on guard to defend his humility against those two great corrupters of men: power and applause.

He has asked the papers to "cut out the flowery adjectives when you write about me and just say, 'the Pope said this or the Pope did that.' " He once stopped in the middle of a speech to ask his audience to forgive him for "unseemly exuberance."

Several Italian newspapers have reported that the Pope intends to abolish the *sedia gestatoria*, the thronelike chair on which he is carried on ceremonial occasions. At a recent ceremony in one of Rome's smaller churches he excused himself from using it by saying, "I don't like riding over the heads of the people."

I had been one of many Canadians who saw him in this ornate conveyance on May 3. He officiated in St. Peter's to beatify Marguerite d'Youville, founder of the Grey Nuns of Montreal, the first Canadian-born person to attain the ranks of the Blessed. I had been dazzled by the baroque splendor, but the ceremony seemed short. A young priest from Winnipeg told me that the Pope had shortened it to half an hour.

Dressed in gorgeous papal vestments and with a jeweled miter on his head, he had been borne in and out of the basilica on "this armchair," as he calls the *sedia gestatoria*, by twelve men. He makes a point of conversing with the men as often as ceremonial permits. It is almost as though he were apologizing for a tradition that demands such a service of them. As I watched his face through opera glasses, it seemed to me he was in the world of pomp but not of it.

He has asked pilgrims not to applaud him, particularly in St. Peter's, but they continue to do so. They applaud him at audiences, but here they are doubtless impelled, as I was, by the relief of tension that follows the embrace of his smile.

He moved among us in a clockwise direction, accompanied by his secretary, Msgr. Loris Capovilla, whose boyish face still wore the traces of the last room's laughter.

"A Canadian!" the Holy Father exclaimed in heavily accented French when at last he faced me. His tone and the way he looked at me made it seem as though this was by far the nicest encounter of his morning. Having mastered what he commends to his flock, "an invincible optimism and a heart open to the genuine effusions of Christian brotherhood," the Pope greets everybody, friend or stranger, like a long-lost and greatly loved relative.

"Rome is full of Canadians now," he continued, as though this were a lucky break for Rome. "Only the other day we beatified one of you. On Monday morning I saw four hundred of you right here." He inclined his head in the general direction of a larger room in which I had been present when he received four hundred Canadians following the beatification of Marguerite d'Youville. "You were there?"

It was not so much a question as a statement of fact. The Pope has a remarkable memory for faces. "That Angelo, he's a smart one," says his younger brother Giuseppe, who still works the family farm near Bergamo. "He never forgets a face, whether he sees it in a congregation, on the street, on in a private interview." At my nod of confirmation the Pope's shoulders hunched in the beginnings of a large chuckle.

"You must be getting tired of seeing me," he said. Then he moved to face the woman beside me.

"Come back in three months and I'll speak to you in English," he told the honeymooners from Leeds. He already speaks French, Greek, Turkish, and Bulgarian, and is familiar with German and Spanish. He has lately added the study of English

8

to the crushing burden of responsibility that forces him to rise every day at 5 A.M. and often work long past his normal bedtime of 10 P.M. Sometimes Vatican officials help him, but not after midnight. "Others must get their sleep," he has decreed.

"All the way from California?" he exclaimed to the woman with the bag of rosaries. "I have friends in San Francisco. I'd like to go there someday."

Remarks like this make Vatican traditionalists extremely nervous. A rumor is current that the Pope would like to travel. Already, in eight months, he has left the Vatican more often than Pius XII did in twenty years. He has visited churches, hospitals, homes for the aged, hostels—and the worst jail in Rome. Here he astonished some observers by removing his skullcap and waving it in farewell. He also told the convicts that one of his cousins had once spent a month in jail for poaching. (This admission the *Osservatore Romano* transformed into "A distant relative transgressed and was duly punished.")

His love of company is evident at an audience. It was plain that he was enjoying himself as much as we were. He loves to talk, particularly about home. When he met a young priest from Bergamo, his home province, he might have gone on indefinitely if it had not been for the anxious glances of Monsignor Capovilla.

His optimism never leaves him. He seemed undisturbed even by the gaunt young priest who was almost the last to be spoken to. The priest, a Czechoslovakian, is an exile in Germany.

"Ah, yes," the Pope replied after listening to his story. "We have come back to the days of the persecution of the Christians, when faith was at its strongest and most beautiful."

When he spoke of communism, a political system which he holds responsible for "the annulment of the human being," his voice remained as cheerful and his face as serene as it was when he promised the nuns from Rimouski he would pray for them if they would do the same for him. The Pope believes with St.

John of the Cross that "disquietude is always vanity." He has made himself a past master of what some people call positive thinking.

Cardinal Urbani, the new patriarch of Venice, says that Pope John's "constant serenity and optimism, while based on a happy temperament, appears to one who has known him for a long time as the fruit of long interior discipline; the fortunate meeting of a lively intelligence with an ardent heart and a tenacious will."

His serenity will remain intact throughout his reign just as it did throughout the half hour or more it took him to speak to all of us, bless our rosaries and medals, and question us about our families. He did this as though he had all the time in the world for us who were, in fact, a mere ripple in the tidal wave of 600,000 people who will have tried to see him before the year is out.

Before leaving, the Pope paused once more in the doorway, opposite the one where he had entered, and looked back. Again his smile enveloped everybody. He raised his hand, half in a blessing and half in a wave.

For a moment it looked as though he might take off his zucchetto and wave it in the air as he had when he said good-bye to the prisoners. But he didn't. He went out as he had come, like a gust of wind, leaving the warmth of his smile behind.

The Wit of Saints

ટ≫

BY PHYLLIS McGINLEY

Saint watching is a delightful occupation but it has its hazards. The worst is having to cut your way through jungles of dull biography before you see the quarry plain. Pre-Renaissance artists used to paint their subjects as if they were quite boneless under the bright clothes.

Pious writers have done the same thing to saints, drawing them all soul and no body. They pose them in plaster attitudes, hands forever uplifted, eyes cast down. They forget that what a reader wants is not a picture, but a motion picture. The stir of life is missing and so is the sound of a natural voice: the sigh of failure, the murmur of discontent, the ripple of laughter. Most of all I miss the laughter.

Yet I am certain it is there. The dedicated watcher, if he listens long enough, can hear it all about him, a delicate tintinnabulation of joyousness as old as sainthood. In forests of virtue the very branches quiver with gentle hilarity. And, staring, one sees the saints shake off their carven poses and begin to move merrily like men and women.

Ignatius Loyola flings up his arms, clicks his heels, and breaks into the Basque national dance to cheer his guest, the melancholy Ortiz. The Poor Clares warble through cloister halls. Francis of Assisi, carried away with pure happiness, tosses a stick over one shoulder, draws another stick like a bow across his imaginary violin, and, so accompanied, carols songs in the French tongue.

During the process of canonization, the Catholic Church demands proof of joy in the candidate. It is a pity that hagiographers have not kept this point more in mind.

The one kind of wit they are willing to grant their saints is the parting shot, as if good temper were admissible only on one's deathbed. I collect such mots gladly, since deathbed jokes are better than no jokes at all. I admire the ladylike nonchalance of Mary Mazzarello, who bantered with the priest giving her the last rites. When he had finished anointing her she looked up and said tartly, "Well, that's my passport. I expect I can leave any time now."

John Berchmans mocked the doctor's prescription for his illness. Indeed, it does sound odd to modern ears since it consisted of bathing the patient's forehead with vintage wine. "A good thing I haven't long to live!" John muttered. "I can't afford such an expensive disease."

And there is always the raillery of Sir Thomas More to add to an anthology of last words. More, "the most virtuous fellow in England," was a good family man. He was also a good friend to Erasmus and all the wits of his day and "the king's good servant but God's first." (It was that final reservation that lost him his head.) He managed to be gay even to the executioner. "Assist me up, if you please," he said with as much aplomb as if he were still in his own home. "Coming down I can shift for myself."

Surely saints who can respond to death in such fashion must also have owned gaiety in their lives!

Now and then one comes across a character so ebullient that it can not be stifled by the dreariest historian. Teresa of Avila, irrepressible as a volcano, unsinkable as balsa wood, never fitted for a moment into a pious straitjacket. "From silly devotions and sour-faced saints, good Lord deliver us!" she protested. And the salt of wit flavors her every action. Besides, she wrote letters endlessly, so her true voice comes through: praising, admonishing, or encouraging, but always with humor. We have her own description of another saint who was her right hand in reforming the Carmelite Order grown lax and luxurious in Spain: the great John of the Cross. John was a tiny man, not five feet tall. Teresa valued him highly, but she couldn't resist making fun of his size. "Isn't it splendid?" she wrote to a friend. "With John here, we now have a monk and a half."

Teresa could not live with pomposity. Self-importance was a balloon she pricked whenever she saw it bobbing along. I relish her advice to a young nun who came to her with tales of exaggerated temptation and who boasted of being a very great sinner.

"Now, Sister," Teresa said deflatingly, "remember, none of us is perfect. Just make sure those sins of yours don't turn into bad habits."

Literary pomposity annoyed her as much as any other kind. After reading some fatuous religious essay by a certain *Señor* Salcedo, she commented, "The man never stops repeating 'As St. Paul says,' 'As the Holy Spirit says,' and then he ends by regretting that he has written nothing but nonsense."

The Basques have a reputation for being taciturn, dry as Vermonters, and Ignatius was a Basque. So he could send Francis Xavier off to India—and Francis was the dearest of his disciples as he was the hardest to win—with no more show of emotion than a handclasp. But he had his own kind of humor and approved of happiness. Like John of Saxony, the good Dominican who said to the novices he found giggling in the seminary, "Keep on laughing, youngsters; it's the way you escape from the devil," Ignatius commended his seminarians for gaiety. "Laugh and grow strong," he told them. He advised sports as well as lessons for them, quite an innovation at a time when students at the Paris colleges were accustomed to rising at five in the morning, studying until nine before they took breakfast, and going on with their books until candles guttered in the evening.

The Ignatian recreation seems to have been billiards and one finds him playing once for a wager. A gentleman who was half thinking of becoming a Jesuit but balked at trying the *Spiritual Exercises*, which were the first step on the journey, dined with him one day. After dinner Ignatius challenged him to a game.

"If I lose, I shall become your servant for a month. If I win, you'll take a month for the *Exercises*."

It is nice to report that the saint beat his friend roundly.

He also enjoyed chess, as did Charles Borromeo. The latter was once criticized for the pleasure he took in his skill.

"And what would you do if you were playing away and the end of the world suddenly arrived?"

"Keep on playing chess," said Borromeo.

The steely Charles was rather an intimidating character, and it is not usual to see him in so light a mood. But then he lived in a dark time, almost as dark as ours. The Reformation had split the world apart. Borromeo had not only to repair its ravages in Italy but to try to root out its causes by reforming his own clergy. It did not leave him much time for games.

Some saints were so jocular that even the Reformation could not dim their good cheer. The most renowned of these was Philip Neri, who along with Borromeo, Pius V, and Loyola, stands as one of the four pillars shouldering the sky when it seemed to be crashing over Europe. By eloquence and personal example they managed to rebuild, reinforce, and shore up religion's foundations, eaten away by corruption.

It's odd about Philip, though. He was so virtuous that the world sanctified him in his lifetime and so genial that the two books he valued most were a New Testament and a volume of jokes and riddles. The *Lives* insist he was a wit. But his biographers seem to have strained out the witticisms and left us only his strange capers. His jokes seem practical jokes, his liveliness mere antics like shaving half his beard and pretending to be tipsy by way of scotching rumors of his holiness. Still, we do know he was the least sour of men and believed like Ludovic Pavone (born delightfully on April Fool's Day) that "rigorism keeps heaven empty."

"I will have no sadness in my house," he told the young men who flocked to his oratory. And he was tirelessly kind to penitents.

"Don't be forever dwelling on your sins," he advised them. "Leave a little something for the angels."

Leaving something for angels is one point on which he might have agreed with his mighty opponent, Martin Luther. Master Martin's close friend was Philip Melancthon, author of the Augsburg *Confessions.* Philip was a cool man where Luther was fervid, a scholar as opposed to a doer, and he continued to live like a monk even after he had joined Luther and left off wearing the tonsure. One day Luther lost patience with Melancthon's virtuous reserve.

"For heaven's sake," he roared, "why don't you go out and sin a little? God deserves to have something to forgive you for!"

Humor in reformers was always a rarity. They tell us that Don John Bosco is celebrated for it, but he is like Philip in having had the essential juice somehow squeezed out of him by historians. He, too, was patron to delinquent boys and, three hundred years after Neri, used Nerian techniques to rescue the homeless young of Rome. (His boys adored him and it is touching to read that one of them, turning a lathe in some factory while John passed by on the pavement, was so eager to reach him that he plunged through the shop door, glass pane and all.) He loved picnics, acrobatics, and "the civilizing effects of good music." Yet though he is called a wit, I find in him chiefly a peasant's rough-and-ready good nature, perfectly suited to the juvenile mind. And his most famous joke is a clown's joke, a Chaplinesque episode.

He had his foes, as reformers will, and they were strong enough to persuade the authorities that the man was a lunatic for trying to take charge of so great a group of children without visible resources. A carriage arrived one day with two priests in it, prepared to carry him off for examination at the hospital. John, however, had been warned. So he was amiable to the Fathers and said, certainly, he would be happy to go with them "for a drive in the country."

He got his hat and coat, prepared to step into the carriage, then suddenly seemed to remember his manners. "After you, Fathers," he said with a flourish.

The two priests seated themselves, whereupon John stepped back and slammed the door smartly, shouting to the driver, "To the asylum." The carriage rattled away.

John, however, could turn a neat phrase when he needed it. "And what sort of habit have you designed for your Order?" asked a literal-minded benefactor when John was attempting, not to found the Salesians, which later became his Order, but simply to rent a building where he could house his strays.

"Why, the habit of virtue, sir," said Don John.

It takes a good deal of eavesdropping and reading between the lines, though, to get at most of the gaiety. We hear that Deicelus "was always smiling" or that Lioba, that intrepid missionary to seventh-century Germany, "had a face like an angel, ever pleasant and laughing," but one can only guess at the humor behind the wonder-working.

Sometimes saints are witty simply by accident. I find it amusing that Good King Wenceslaus of the ballad is listed in the calendar along with his daughter. I think it diverting that St. Vitus is patron not of the dance but of those who, like me, have trouble getting up early in the morning; and that Benedict of Amiane began his career as cupbearer to Charlemagne. Indeed, it seems to me comic that Charlemagne himself was long ago beatified. What heaven makes of that warlike and half-pagan old conqueror one can only surmise. But he won the title of "blessed" long before canonization became an official Church function and when it was a shabby hero or an amazingly incompetent bishop who did not make the lists by local acclaim.

For that matter, the great Jerome, Doctor of the Church and first translator of the Bible into Latin, often seems uneasy among the holy congregation. A fiercer man never lived to drive the Desert Fathers mad with argument. Yet no one can deny his wit. It was wit of a deadly brand, killing as a sword. One sees it at work in his letters to Augustine, himself no mean opponent. He uses it as a weapon against heresy, the heresy which often seems any doctrine with which Jerome did not agree.

Poor Rufinus lives forever pilloried in the screed the fiery Doctor wrote against him when they got into an argument over the theories of Origen. Jerome not only demolished Rufinus' case, he demolished Rufinus. He describes the poor fellow's "tortoise walk," the way he cracked his fingers and beamed when he was about to make a telling point for an audience, his little grunts and hiccoughs and classroom mannerisms.

Still, there is another side to Jerome, when the old lion turns gentle and merely smiles at another saint, Fabiola, whose nature was so sociable that she could not bear to be without company. "Her idea of the Stable is that it should be an annex to the Inn," he says with perfect good temper.

Nearly as sociable as Fabiola was Pius X, although as Pontiff at the turn of the century he had little enough time to indulge that side of his sunny nature. He did make one endearing innovation as soon as he came to the Vatican. It had been a long-standing custom there for Popes to take their meals alone. Pius would have none of the stately tradition. He dined with his relatives, friends, and visiting priests; he ate with messengers, aides, the workmen in his gardens. Not even the crushing weight of the tiara could quench his gregariousness. What did quench it for a time was hearing that people had begun to call him a saint and were counting up his miracles.

"So now it's miracles they want from me," he burst out. "As if I didn't have enough to do already!"

Pius belongs to our modern age, so he is not hard to spy on. As a saint watcher, though, I find the sport more exhilarating when I can come across some unexpected flash of color in a somber copse, or catch a small domestic glimpse of holy people at play. I enjoy listening to the comment of the Little Poor Man who, after lodging for a while at the house of a certain Cardinal Leo, went home and caught an ague so painful that he swore he had been beaten by the devil.

"Which is my punishment," said Francis, "for consorting with cardinals."

I cherish the little scene at table with Thomas More, the same Thomas who contrived a joke with his executioner. More had trained for sainthood long before he fell into the bad graces of Henry VIII, and always practiced secret austerities. The secret came out one day at dinner with his family. He had taken off his ruff for comfort, when, eyeing him, his daughter-in-law fell into giggles.

As the rest of the company followed her pointing finger, they caught the hysteria. More looked down at himself and began to laugh as loudly as they. Then he hastily and shamefacedly stuffed back under his doublet the hairshirt which had been nudging itself into sight.

I love his brand of unself-conscious piety as I admire Madeleine Sophie Barat's retort to a disapproving letter. Madeleine Sophie was a great teacher, a great lady, and a Frenchwoman to the bone. She founded the Society of the Sacred Heart, and the Madames of that aristocratic order still educate young women all over the world. (The present Crown Princess of Japan was once a Sacred Heart pupil in Tokyo and I would lay a small bet that to this day she remembers how to curtsy on a staircase with a load of books in her arms as well as she knows how to conjugate a Latin verb. The curtsy is a Sacred Heart specialty along with the classics.) Mother Barat lived before Jane Austen but there is a touch of Austen in her tone when she rebukes the popinjay who had suggested resentfully that French girls in her schools were aping the curriculum reserved for French gentlemen.

"Our Society," she wrote, "has not been established to prove that women can become men, even though that may be easy in a country where so many men become women."

The female saints seem often to be sharper-mannered than the men; or perhaps they are merely franker in their letters. I discover male saints so incapable of malice that one wonders how they managed to survive in this imperfect world. John of Vercelli found it impossible to frown and had to insist that his *socius*, or aide in the Dominican Order, should be "of severe and awe-inspiring countenance." Anthony Grasse could not bear to hear an angry syllable.

But when I am searching for the elusive accent of wit, I can always return to Teresa of Avila. Mystic that she was, she lived in such astonishing communication with God that they carried on conversations in which God sometimes sounds very much like Teresa. Nearly everyone knows her famous comment made to Him in an exasperated moment when all her plans seemed failing and her reform impossible.

"No wonder You have so few friends," she told Him with spirit, "When You treat the ones You have so badly."

Not so familiar is the scrap of dialogue she records at a time when one of her recalcitrant abbesses was being particularly tiresome. "Lord," she prayed, "if I had my way that woman wouldn't be Superior here."

And God answered her as wryly. "Teresa," He said, "if I had my way, she wouldn't be either."

Overhearing, I am reassured. Wit is not the prerogative of the unjust; there is laughter in holy places.

The Roots of the World

 famo

BY G. K. CHESTERTON

Once upon a time a little boy lived in a garden in which he was permitted to pick the flowers but forbidden to pull them up by the roots. There was, however, one particular plant, insignificant, somewhat thorny, with a small, starlike flower, which he very much wanted to pull up by the roots.

His tutors and guardians, who lived in the house with him, were worthy, formal people, and they gave him reasons why he should not pull it up. They were silly reasons as a rule. But none of the reasons against doing the thing was quite so silly as the little boy's reason for wanting to do it; for his reason was that Truth demanded that he should pull the thing up by the roots to see how it was growing. Still, it was a sleepy, thoughtless kind of house and nobody gave him the real answer to his argument, which was that it would kill the plant and that there is no more Truth about a dead plant than about a live one.

So one dark night, when clouds sealed the moon like a secret too good or too bad to be told, the little boy came down the old creaking stairs of his farmhouse and crept into the garden in his nightgown. He told himself repeatedly that there was no more reason against his pulling this plant than against his knocking off a thistletop idly in a lane. Yet the darkness which he had chosen contradicted him, and also his own throbbing pulse.

When he laid hold of the little plant in the garden he tugged and tugged and found the thing held as if clamped to the earth with iron. And when he strained himself a third time there came a frightful noise behind him and either nerves or (which he would have denied) conscience made him leap back and stagger and stare around. The house he lived in was a mere bulk of blackness against a sky almost as black. Yet, after staring long he saw that the very outline had grown unfamiliar, for the great chimney of the kitchen had fallen crooked and calamitous.

Desperately he gave another pull at the plant and heard far off the roof of the stables fall in and the horses shriek and plunge. Then he ran into the house and rolled himself in the bedclothes.

Next morning found the kitchen ruined, the day's food destroyed, two horses dead, and three broken loose and lost. But the boy still kept a furious curiosity and a little while after, when a fog from the sea had hidden house and garden, he dragged again at the roots of the indestructible plant.

He hung on to it like a boy on the rope of a tug of war, but it did not give. Only through the gray sea fog came choking and panic-stricken cries; they cried that the king's castle had fallen, that the towers guarding the coast were gone, that half the great sea city had slid into the sea.

Then the boy was frightened for a little while and said no more about the plant, but when he had come to a strong and careless manhood, and the desruction in the district had been slowly repaired, he said openly before the people, "Let us have done with the riddle of this irrational weed. In the name of Truth let us drag it up."

22

He gathered a great company of strong men, like an army to meet invaders, and they all laid hold of the little plant and they tugged night and day. And the Great Wall fell down in China for forty miles. And the Pyramids were split into jagged stones. And the Eiffel Tower in Paris went over like a ninepin, killing half the Parisians; and the Statue of Liberty in New York Harbor fell forward suddenly and smashed the American fleet; and St. Paul's Cathedral killed all the journalists in Fleet Street; and Japan had a record series of earthquakes and then sank into the sea.

When they had tugged for about twenty-four hours the strong men of that country had pulled down about half of the civilized world, but had not pulled up the plant. I will not weary the reader with the full facts of this realistic story, with how they used first elephants and then steam engines to tear up the flower, and how the only result was that the flower stuck fast, but that the moon began to be agitated and even the sun was a bit dicky.

At last the human race interfered, as it always does at last, by means of a revolution. But long before that the boy, or man, who is the hero of this tale, had thrown up the business, saying to his pastors and masters, "You gave me a number of elaborate and idle reasons why I should not pull up this shrub. Why did you not give me the two good reasons: 1. that I can't; 2. that I should damage everything else if I tried?"

All those who have sought to uproot religion seem to me very like the little boy in the garden. Skeptics do not succeed in pulling up the roots of Christianity; but they do succeed in pulling up the roots of every man's ordinary vine and fig tree, of every man's garden and every man's kitchen garden. Secularists have not succeeded in wrecking divine things; but secularists have succeeded in wrecking secular things.

℞ FOR THE BLUES

I know a businessman, who, whenever someone comes to his office bemoaning his misfortunes in business, love, or life, takes him aside to a framed, hand-lettered sign hanging on the wall.

Failed in business,	'31
Defeated for legislature,	'32
Failed in business again,	'33
Elected to legislature,	'34
Sweetheart died,	'35
Suffered nervous breakdown,	'36
Defeated for speaker,	'38
Defeated for elector,	'40
Defeated for Congress,	'43
Elected to Congress,	'46
Defeated for Congress,	'48
Defeated for Senate,	'55
Defeated for Vice President,	'56
Defeated for Senate,	'58
Elected President of United States,	'60

The person who made this record of misfortune, crowned by final success, was Abraham Lincoln.

Thomas P. Ramirez.

RUSSIAN ROULETTE

During Nikita Khrushchev's sweetness-and-light visit in 1959 a reception was being held for American visitors in the Russian consulate in San Francisco.

While we waited for Nikita to make his appearance, the scene inside the Soviet hall became one of the greatest roughhouses I have ever beheld. Reporters and visitors alike were shouting and scrapping with each other. Cameramen fought, jostled, and pushed for better vantage points. The din was at its height when Khrushchev finally appeared.

In the sudden hush that settled over the room at the Russian's entrance a television cameraman could be heard distinctly above the loud silence. He was bawling out someone. ". . . and furthermore," he said, "you are the biggest idiot I have ever seen in my life!"

"Silence!" commanded a Russian guard. "Don't forget that Chairman Khrushchev is present!"

Edmund Forbes Burke.

ARTISTS' LIFE

The late Fritz Kreisler, the great violinist, was walking down the street one day with a friend and the two stopped to look in the window of a shop. A fine catch of fish, mouths open and eyes staring, were ranged in a display.

Kreisler suddenly clutched his friend by the arm. "Great heavens!" he exclaimed. "That reminds me—I should be playing at a concert!"

Jim Kelly.

Two young men stopped before an exhibit of modern art at the Guggenheim Museum in New York City. One particular picture seemed to hold their attention.

"I think I can understand most of it," one remarked. "But that funny-looking spot right in the center has me baffled."

"Me, too," replied the other. "Let's get out of here quick before they think that one of us did it!"

Spice Box.

I.D. CARD

Our correspondents report that in darkest America it has become customary in some quarters to carry in wallet or purse a card which reads: "I am an important Catholic. In case of serious illness or accident, please call a bishop."

London Tablet.

RANK WILL TELL

The college professor was annoyed when a student fresh out of the Army was late to class for the third straight time. "Glad you could make it," the prof observed sarcastically. "Tell me, what did they say in the Army when you showed up late like this?"

"Well," the student replied, "first they saluted. Then they asked, 'How are you this morning, sir?'"

Dr. L. Binder.

THE GOOD COMPANIONS

A young Air Force second lieutenant was to appear before a selection board convened to interview applicants for higher commissions. He spent the whole previous evening shining his shoes, polishing his brass, and trying to anticipate the questions he might be asked.

When he entered the board room he was prepared for anything—except the unusually high door sill. He fell flat on his face before the astonished officers. The lieutenant picked himself up, dusted himself off, and observed, "Well, at least I fell into good company."

He received his promotion.

True.

26

No wonder the teen-ager of today is confused. It often seems to him that half the adults are telling him to "find himself," while the other half are telling him to "get lost."

Morris Bender.

THE PROPER BOSTONIANS

Young Terwillingham had been enrolled in an exclusive private school in Boston. His mother was much given to bragging about her son's academic affiliations until one bright day on which she received an acid communication from Terwillingham's teacher demanding a written excuse for his presence.

Changing Times.

*

A lady tourist visiting Boston was reprimanded by a policeman when she failed to halt for a stop sign at an intersection. She protested that in her home town, "We just slow down and look in both directions."

"In Boston, madam," the policeman replied, " 'Stop' means an absolute cessation of all forward movement."

Charles Kennedy.

STOREHOUSE

A proud alumnus once congratulated President Charles W. Eliot on all that he had done to make Harvard a great storehouse of knowledge.

"Yes," he replied ruefully, "I think we can say that Harvard now is indeed a great storehouse of knowledge. But sometimes I think it is so only because our freshmen bring so much knowledge in and our seniors take so little out."

Quote.

27

WORK SUSPENDED

Senator Dirksen of Illinois tells of a member of the House of Representatives who was awakened in the night by his wife. "Get up, John," she insisted. "There are burglars in the house."

"Burglars in the House? Impossible!" the congressman replied. "In the Senate, perhaps, but never in the House."

Chicago Tribune.

CRITIC ON THE HEARTH

Historians have sometimes portrayed George Washington as a man without humor. But he seems to have been able to hold his own in the art of repartee.

Once, as he sat at the table after dinner, he complained that the fire in the fireplace behind him was too large and hot.

"But, sir," rejoined a guest, "surely it behooves a general to withstand fire!"

"Yes," replied Washington, "but it does not become him to receive it from the rear."

Mrs. S. Lee.

THE LONER

Said of Sir Stafford Cripps by Winston Churchill: "He could see a joke only by appointment."

The New York Times.

COUNTLESS IN PRINCETON

Few people remember, if they ever knew, that the late Albert Einstein was an amateur violinist. Once, during the time that Dr.

28

Einstein was at the Institute for Advanced Study in Princeton, he was visited by Jascha Heifetz, Gregor Piatigorski, and Artur Rubinstein. They suggested that Einstein join them in a little chamber music. The scientific genius was thrilled. He quickly produced his violin and the group began a delicate Mozart quartet. After a few moments Rubinstein looked up in annoyance. "My dear Dr. Einstein," he demanded, "what's wrong with you? Can't you count?"

Spice Box.

EYE WASH

Oliver St. John Gogarty, Ireland's great physician and poet, was also a great punster. Walking into a tavern one day, he saw a friend wearing a patch over one eye and couldn't resist saying, "Drink to me with thine only eye."

Pageant.

FLIGHTS OF FANCY

A toiling, sweating sun stoked the sky—*F. Scott Fitzgerald.*
Two pessimists meeting to shake heads—*Scott Brady.*
So henpecked his wife wouldn't let him smoke a thinking man's
    filter—*Sam Levenson.*
Salesman: a man with a smile on his face, a shine on his shoes,
    and a lousy territory—*George Gobel.*
Flop: the flip side of a hit record—*Louise Baer.*
Coming to gripes with reality—*Morris Bender.*
The broom-swish of her voice—*Sinclair Lewis.*

II THE CLOTH

Illustration from *Eight Nuns in an Austin*

Five Nuns at a Bullfight

ც঵

BY SISTER MARY CORDE LORANG

Huehuetenango, in Guatemala, goes by the nickname of Huehue, pronounced *way-way*. It is a likable small pueblo, the capital of a sparsely inhabited mountain state.

Sister Albert showed me around town. She had been a teacher in Clarence County, New York, then a missioner in up-country China for nineteen years until the communists took over. Since then she has spent fourteen years in Bolivia, Panama, and Guatemala.

The Maryknoll Fathers have spiritual care of this state. One of the big difficulties is the inaccessibility of the towns. To go to Jacaltenango, for instance, takes four hours by jeep and then five hours on horseback. The Maryknoll center at Huehue keeps in touch with many missions only by ham radio.

Brother Carl drove up in a jeep. He was elated that he had won second prize at the agricultural fair just then going on in the city. Brother has been introducing new crops; his experimental farm has raised the nourishment level of the area to a new high.

33

We continued down Main Street, past the long, gray city hospital, now under the direction of the Incarnate Word Sisters. A vision out of a First World War poster strode toward us. A tall, good-looking Indian in red striped pants and short blue jacket. "We call them Uncle Sam boys," Sister Albert laughed. "They are the Indians from Todos Santos, miles away from Huehue, but they bring their products here to be sold."

Many Indians passed us. Sister identified each from his costume. "He's from San Rafael. That one's from San Sebastian. There's an Indian from La Democracia."

A hullabaloo across the street made me turn as red-headed James Reed, a Peace Corps worker, came toward me. Stopping short just before he ran me down, he waited to catch his breath and then introduced a short, dark man, muscular and quick.

"My friend, Alfonso Paez from Colombia," Jim said. "He's a matador, here for the bullfights next Sunday."

I raised my eyes to an ad posted on the wall. Yes, it said, "BULLFIGHT, Saturday 2 P.M."

"Sunday?" I questioned.

"Sunday," Alfonso said.

"The ad says Saturday," I objected.

"No. I will fight on Sunday, ad or no ad."

"Why?" asked matter-of-fact Sister Albert.

Alfonso shrugged his shoulders. "Why? Well, it just is." And that was that.

Once he had been a seminarian, Alfonso said, but "I am much better at fighting bulls than at praying."

Well, there was once a novice in England, I remember, who had left the convent to go lion taming.

"Have you a piece of paper?" he continued. "I will write you something with my name." We did not look too hard to find one. I am not an autograph collector, not even of matadors' autographs.

34

That evening two of the muddiest Sisters I ever saw came into the convent. Sister Rose Cordis and Sister Bernice Marie, doctor and nurse, had been riding horseback for twelve hours down the muddy trail from their hospital in Jacaltenango.

They had come to pick up native woolen blankets at the fair. Also medical supplies and pans. The two of them sat around our table, chatting, figuring out how much they could buy, and how they would stow it on their horses or on pack animals.

I marveled at what they have done out there in their small mountain hospital. They are the doctor and nurse who worked all through a night to rejoin a child's foot to her leg. It was hanging by three-eighths of an inch of skin when the mother brought them her eighteen-month-old baby from a nearby village. A similar case, involving a boy's arm, had occurred in Boston not long before. But there a team of doctors and nurses had worked with all the modern facilities of a large hospital. In Jacaltenango the lone doctor and nurse worked with a kerosene lamp and few instruments. The child runs now like any other youngster.

Saturday we plunged into the past. A twenty-minute drive through peaceful grazing land surrounded by rugged peaks took us back fifteen hundred years.

"Look at that," Sister Maria Esperanza said. We stood on a mountain curve with a wide, verdant plateau spread below us. Lifting their heads above the large trees were snow-white temples.

"Zaculeu, isn't it?" I asked. This was the Mayan city the United Fruit Company restored, hiring the famous archaeologist John M. Dimick to direct the work.

The road dipped down to the plateau. As we entered the ancient city, not a soul was in sight. It seemed strange to be alone here, almost as if we had wandered out of the past. The Mayas, we thought, might come back at any moment to welcome us to their empty stronghold. The restoration is complete; each stone is in place. Even the original workmen could not have done more perfect work.

"According to the investigations carried on by the United Fruit Company," Sister said, "Zaculeu was flourishing in the fourth century A.D., and, of course, it must have been founded earlier."

A pyramid temple dominates the plaza. It is made up of nine receding layers and crowned by a severely plain temple, almost early Grecian in proportion. A flight of some forty to fifty steep, narrow steps climbed up one side.

A large ball court is at the left, two long, sloping walls with ample space on top for spectators. Stairways at the ends make it easy to climb up to the viewing stands.

Beyond this is a dainty building something like a low pyramid. Again, the summit is crowned by a temple which relied on its proportion for beauty, rather than on ornamentation. Slender, plain columns form doorways.

"I always call that the Greek temple," said Sister Maria Esperanza. "Last month I brought the Girl Scouts here on an outing, and when the rain burst upon us we took refuge up there in the shelter. It was a thrill to look out at the cloudburst through those lovely openings."

Back at the convent, Sister Albert met us with news. We would go to the fair that afternoon, even though it was raining. Also, she held a large white envelope. In it was a nice bevel-edged card with fancy lettering to the effect that the two of us and three other Sisters were invited to attend the bullfight, as guests of Alfonso Paez, matador from Colombia, Sunday, at 2 P.M., at the football stadium.

"It's the chance of a lifetime!" Sister Maria Esperanza exulted. She is a native of Ecuador; it had been a long time since she had seen a bullfight. The other Sisters had their reservations.

"Must be terribly bloody." "My parents saw one in Mexico City. They were jittery for days afterward." "Sisters don't go to bullfights. Just as they don't go to prize fights in the States."

The Ecuadorian had some good arguments. "In the big cities, no, we do not go. But this is part of the background of our people. Besides, this is the first bullfight Huehue ever had. It will be very tame."

"Let the idea simmer until tomorrow," said the wisest among us. "We'll see how the fair goes, first." Two o'clock, and pouring rain. But thousands of people were milling around the booths.

Father William Woods stood proudly beside his collection of native woods. He had arranged small pieces in an attractive design which had won first prize. The whole collection of beautiful woods seemed to shout, "This is one of your resources. Let's use it!"

Brother Carl's exhibit of maize, vegetables, coffee, was not only a winner, but also an education to the Indians passing by. Many people from other areas of Huehuetenango State remarked, "Do you suppose we could get Brother to help us a bit?"

To get background for the bullfight decision we went around to the football stadium. Looking in, I envisioned a brave matador and ferocious bull. "Where could he hide? It is a long way to the fence."

Sister Esperanza pooh-poohed the idea. "These bulls are the dinner-table kind. They won't get really mad."

Sunday morning we made up our collective mind. We would go and try to absorb a little more of Guatemala's culture.

Sister Maria Esperanza was calculating. "Let's see. It's advertised to start at two. It won't, of course. But this is Huehue's first bullfight, so a lot of people will be going. To get good seats we ought to be very early. We should get there by two fifteen."

We did and we were first in line by a long, long shot. Through the wire fence we could see a few men inside, leisurely nailing boards together to make a sort of chicken coop. "Probably an enclosure for the bulls," Sister Maria Esperanza said, "although that thing is too flimsy even for dogs."

We walked around the corner and found the bulls in a pen, packed like sardines, but very patient about it all. There were seven, two for each of the three matadors and one extra. It gave me the creeps to look at these inoffensive animals who, in a few hours would all be dead. Ah! Little did I know.

Two forty-five. Back we went to the ticket office. No claimers for first place yet. We settled down to wait it out. Soon others came and formed a line.

"Where are the tickets?" I asked.

"Probably in the matadors' pockets," our Ecuadorian Sister said. "Usually neither the city officials nor the matadors trust one another."

Enter a mystery woman. A tall brunette, dressed in black, escorted by two male editions of the same, came by. The three of them walked here and there, passing back and forth, eyeing us, and yet trying desperately to ignore us.

"Who's she?" I asked.

"Not local," said Sister Albert.

The crowd behind us was growing fast. They were always pushing, so one more shove did not matter much. Then we saw Alfonso Paez beside us. He greeted us warmly; we thanked him for the passes.

Sister Albert, with the carnage of the bullfight drawing closer, murmured, "And we'll pray for your safety."

38

"Thank you, Sister," he replied with a far-off look. "I will need it today."

He introduced his friend, a tall lean matador known as El Seville, directly from Spain. Both wore rose-colored outfits, lavishly embroidered in gold, tight as their skins, and far too gorgeous to wear to a bloody old bullfight.

Alfonso pounded on the door beside the ticket booth. Eventually a man with a key wobbled over the field to open it. Plainly he had fortified himself for the afternoon's ordeal. As the two matadors entered the arena Alfonso turned to let me take a picture of him.

"I hope that won't be the last picture he ever has taken," Sister Albert moaned.

The two matadors did have the tickets with them. They went to the ticket windows to instruct the sellers. But still no one would sell tickets.

Three thirty. The crowd surged forward again. The cause was the third matador. A short, thin fellow from Guatemala, he was dressed in blue satin bedecked with gold. He strode up to the gate before us and pounded again and again. No result. He threw his arms out, struck his breast and shouted, "I am a matador! I am here to fight the bulls. Let me at those bulls!"

Sister Maria Esperanza looked through the crowd behind us, saw one of her Boy Scouts, and motioned to him to squeeze his way to us. We locked our heads together and hoisted him over the eight-foot fence.

"Find the gatekeeper. Tell him to open the door and let the matador in," she said.

The lad scrambled down the other side of the fence and ran for the gatekeeper. In ten minutes he was back.

"He's out cold," he reported.

"Then go tell Alfonso and the other matador," Sister said.

39

"Tell them to put the gatekeeper on his feet and propel him to the door. They can hold his hand until the gate is opened." Which is just what they did.

Four o'clock. Blueboy slipped through the gate and so did the woman in black and her two guards. They all went straight to the ticket booth.

"Now the tickets will be sold." The man at my left breathed out his relief.

"Why, now?" I asked.

"Ah, you do not know. The matadors brought the tickets. The town officials do not trust the matadors. The matadors do not trust the town officials. All want their share of the money. And that lady in black, nobody trusts her. Now they are all together. Business will begin."

He was right. The ticket windows flew up. The gates opened and we entered. In the mad stampede for the roofed-over stands on either side of the center field we managed to use elbows to good advantage and secured places on the fourth bench up.

Five o'clock. The crowds overflowed the seats and stood in a solid mass behind the wire which separated the arena from the bleachers. Every tree, window, and wall overlooking the stadium was jammed with freeloaders. The woman in black and the two men crossed the field from one side to the other, bent on some inscrutable purpose. No one greeted them; they spoke to no one.

Five fifteen. By now the crowd was so jammed up against the doors that it was impossible to bring the bulls into the stadium. So the management decided to open a large boarded-up double door in the center. With hammer and machete they pried off the boards. Even then the door, large enough to admit a house trailer, would not swing. Ah, a crowbar! Pushing mightily on the door and using the crowbar as a lever, they strained and panted. At last! The rusted hinges broke and the whole half-door fell with a crash.

This posed a problem. The bull could now get in, but how to keep him in? It was solved easily. Seven men on horseback had gone out with a flourish and brought in one bewildered bull. After he wandered in, two men stood at either side of the gaping hole and held a plank across it. This would keep the ferocious bull inside the arena.

The inoffensive animal patiently permitted himself to be tied to a slat in the enclosure they had batted together that afternoon. The matadors started practicing passes at the tied-up bull. El Seville got a little close. The bull lunged and El Seville sprinted up a fence.

Then Blueboy made a few passes with his *capa*. The bull twisted his head and captured the *capa* on one horn. Blueboy took to his heels.

Sister Albert put her hands over her eyes. "I'm not going to look. Don't tell me what's happening, either. I only want to know when it's all over."

Alfonso was waiting for the bull to be free. For what seemed an age, probably five minutes, they eyed each other. The spectators eyed them. The guards at the broken door eyed the situation and noted means of exit. It was a scene of frozen waiting.

There came a mighty roar, a violent lunge. The bull yanked off the plank he was tied to and trotted into the arena with a blue *capa* draped roguishly on one horn and a plank tied round his neck. All three matadors pushed back as far as they could go. The men at the broken door stood on one foot ready to sprint elsewhere. The horsemen edged away with their horses. The audience held its collective breath.

The bull strolled to the center of the field, looked over the spectators, and leisurely walked toward the door, flipping the *capa* jauntily and dragging his plank.

The men at the door dropped their plank and ran in opposite directions. The horsemen fidgeted. The matadors ran to intercept their adversary but he had a head start. As he neared the exit he tossed the *capa* off and the plank slid out of the rope, so he picked up speed. After him a furious parade poured out the broken door, horsemen, matadors, guards, and spectators. In the commotion a woman and her four offspring slipped through the gate free!

Six thirty. We started for home. The bullfight would fizzle out into a lynching perhaps? Muttered threats boded ill for the matadors.

Just outside the gate we found a pretty situation. A horseman had lassoed the bull. Suddenly violent protests came down from the leafy branches. Five men had scrambled up there. Their safety spot turned out to be a hot spot.

Amid yells from below and yells from above, the bull's head was tied tightly to one side of the trunk while the five refugees slid nervously down the other side of it. Laughing and clapping, we spectators found it the best part of the show.

The three matadors now walked around to the pen to choose another bull. El Seville would fight this one. Which one did he want? That one away back in the rear. The attendants looked annoyed. How to get one bull out of a pen crowded with six, however, was their problem, not his.

They solved it brilliantly. How about letting the first five out and then catching the last one? A first-rate idea. The only flaw was that, once the gate was open, all six made a prison break at high speed. In a matter of seconds only the horsemen and the three matadors were left in the bull pen.

A howl went up from the spectators. The howl reechoed

round the field; it went from bleachers to bleachers; it grew to an angry roar. The crowd surged onto the field.

"What's the idea?" "Beat them up!" "The gyps!" "Hanging's too good."

The police surrounded the matadors and they crawled off to the local jail until the crowd dispersed. Then they went to the local hotel for the night.

By that time the crowd had something else to ponder. All the ticket money was stolen. The finger of suspicion rested on the lady in black and her two escorts. The town officials thought she was employed by the matadors, and the matadors thought she was working for the officials. In the end both came to the conclusion that she was a city slicker working for herself.

A Chat with Ronald Knox

ह‍‍‍‍‍ॐ

BY A. R. McELWAIN

I was an avid fan of the late Msgr. Ronald Knox from the days of my youth in New Zealand and Australia. I admit that I was first attracted by his lighter efforts in literature, like his delicious *On Getting There*. In 1949 I went to work in London's Fleet Street. By then I hoped for nothing more than to meet the man I felt I had known, in a sense, most of my life.

Early in 1950 I wrote to Monsignor Knox to tell him just that. I added that I could meet him "anywhere and at any time" that suited him. He was then living in the Manor House, in Mells, Frome, Somerset—the home of a devoted friend, Mrs. Raymond Asquith. (That is where he died, on August 24, 1957.)

His reply came in March, 1950. Anyone who has read other letters by him will recognize the style as "pure Knox."

I'm never in London if I can help it and consequently when I am my time gets terribly booked up. If you could call at Westminster Cathedral Clergy House about twenty minutes or a quarter of an hour before seven on Sunday next I could pop down for a few minutes in the middle of mugging up my sermon. The clergy house is in Francis Street, behind the east end of the cathedral. I'm sorry to take you so much at your word.

Yours sincerely,

R. A. Knox

I got to the cathedral so early that I decided to walk around its extensive block a few times before going to the clergy house. Westminster Cathedral is hard by Victoria Station. As I was perambulating I saw the thin, stooped, scholarly figure I had until then seen only in pictures.

He was heading from the station, carrying a suitcase. It struck me then as typical of his faith in the English way of things that he anticipated no breakdown in the British railways system that might land him in London late for his sermon—or perhaps not get him there at all.

After introducing myself, I insisted against his wish on carrying the suitcase. He said it was "really awfully good of me."

At the clergy house a maid asked the celebrated churchman his name. He said simply, "Knox." She gave him one of those "never-heard-of-you" looks at which English servants excel. So in the interest of time the humble priest was forced to add "*Monsignor* Knox." It left the girl all of a flutter.

We talked in the study of the cathedral administrator, Msgr. Cuthbert Collingwood. "You will, of course, not interview me," Knox had said. Monsignor Collingwood came in and gave us each a glass of sherry. We talked of Australia, and the war, and somehow the subject of food parcels came up.

Monsignor Knox said he had been much touched by perfect strangers, in Australia and elsewhere, who merely because they had read his books or "knew a little about him as a priest" had sent him parcels during Britain's stringent rationing period. (Monsignor Collingwood capped this by revealing that he had

45

himself been singled out by the Collingwood Football club, a leading Melbourne team, who had seen his name in a Catholic directory and adopted him as their namesake. "They not only sent me food parcels, but an annual report on how they had done during the football season," he told us. Knox thought this very funny.)

I steered Monsignor Knox to the subject of detective stories, explaining that, like many other enthusiasts, I had long adopted the pose of an irregular Baker Street Irregular and worshiped at the shrine of Sherlock Holmes. I knew the Ronald Knox Ten Commandments of Detection: "All supernatural or preternatural agencies are ruled out as a matter of course"; "No more than one secret room or passage is allowable"; "The detective must not himself commit the crime"; and so on. I had also read his own erudite detective stories, like *Still Dead, The Footsteps at the Loch,* and *The Body in the Silo.* Here, I thought, must be a dedicated fellow addict.

I was brutally shaken when he told me that, far from being dedicated, he had turned to writing detective stories for the base reason that he needed money. I have found confirmation of what he told me on this subject in Evelyn Waugh's fine life of Ronald Knox. Mr. Waugh points out that when Knox was Catholic chaplain at Oxford, chaplains' stipends at Oxford and Cambridge were inadequate. It was understood that only priests with other sources of income could hold posts of that kind.

So during his chaplaincy Monsignor Knox wrote five detective stories, the "most impersonal, and for that reason the least exacting form of popular writing" for him, says Mr. Waugh.

Knowing that Monsignor Knox still had to "mug up" his sermon for the crowded congregation that inevitably faced him wherever he preached, I left the clergy house after one of the most pleasant half hours I had ever experienced. I managed to get a standing-room-only position in the back of huge West-

minster Cathedral and heard him preach brilliantly on his be-
loved St. Paul.

As I was leaving the cathedral, I overheard one obvious young
Oxford gentleman address another obvious young Oxford
gentleman as he surveyed the huge crowd shuffling toward the
doors. "I say, Peter, old chap," he drawled, "I can't recollect
ever seeing so many Anglicans in church at one time before."
How convert Knox, many of whose intellectual Anglican
disciples were ever faithful to him, would have loved that!

My last letter from Monsignor Knox came after I had sent
him an advance copy of a collection of American detective
stories edited by Ellery Queen. He wrote on August 3, 1950.
The envelope was addressed to A. R. McEuuuuut, Esq., and the
letter, a little more legibly, to Dear Mr. McEwant. You will see
why.

The awful thing is that, although I can remember you and your
coming round to have a drink at the cathedral, your name has gone
from my memory, and your signature gives no help. I know there
is a difficulty about pronouncing it, but that wouldn't matter if I
could spell it. Forgive me—

Thank you awfully for sending me the Ellery Queen book, which
cheered me up through last week when I was giving a clergy retreat.
I think the Americans are too ingenious about the *story* and don't
quite give you your money's worth in the way of *mystery*. But then
I'm old-fashioned and like a plan of the room with a X to mark
where the paper-knife lay.

It's very kind of you anyhow.

> Yours v. sincerely,
> R. A. Knox

That "it's very kind of you anyhow" came back and hit me
hard when I read Mr. Waugh's moving account of Ronald
Knox's last moments on earth.

47

A good friend, Lady Eldon, knowing he was dying, had come to stay at the Manor House to be near when the end came. Mrs. Asquith and she took turns watching at the bedside. Knox lay in a coma for three days. Once Lady Eldon, detecting a slight return of consciousness, asked him if he would like her to read to him from his own translation of the New Testament. He replied with a faint "No." Then, just as Lady Eldon thought he had fallen into the coma again, "there came from the deathbed, just audibly, in the idiom of his youth, 'Awfully jolly of you to suggest it, though.' " Those were his last words.

Eight Nuns in an Austin

ৰ্≉

BY BERNARD BASSET, S.J.

Officially nuns had no place in the first session of the Second Vatican Council; they were not consulted about Revelation and if they had been would have made no reply. Behind the scenes, however, Sisters labored without ceasing. They nursed, sewed, cooked, scrubbed, and even ran the post office just inside the Vatican arcade.

The Sisters looked sweet and innocent, but all who knew Rome intimately warned us that they were not so green. Full habits and long sleeves concealed their inner strength. (Some said that they carried knives, but I saw no evidence of that.)

Nuns all push or pull together and thus achieve the force of a tug-o'-war team. In the surging crowds in St. Peter's and its piazza the Sisters rode like corks. They never raised their eyes, they spoke in whispers, and looked as meek as St. Gemma Galgani, but got there just the same.

Could it happen that the Swiss Guards, the Palatine Guards, the Noble Guards, the gendarmes, and monsignori all have sisters or aunts in convents and know that it is wise to give way gracefully? Seminarians were caught, middle-aged priests like myself were rounded up, cordoned off and lassoed in hundreds, but I never saw anyone ask a nun how she managed to reach the front seat.

As the bishops left, the Sisters moved in. I saw them sitting in the bishops' seats, testing the voting system; on their knees looking under the conciliar stalls. "I told you, Mother, they are just held with drawing pins," drawled an Australian Sister to her Reverend Mother, seated on a cardinal's throne above.

Out in the piazza we faced a further challenge from nuns on wheels. Few bishops will forget the traffic jams on the ways outside St. Peter's as forty-six buses packed with prelates debouched into the Roman streets. Pigeons circled, the faithful cheered, journalists hunted around for gossip, tourists waved handkerchiefs and begged for blessings while the nuns packed themselves into their little cars. Eight full-grown nuns in an Austin was the then record, but by now this will have been many times exceeded.

Usually I went home on foot but a theologian had offered me a lift when the session was over, and I climbed in outside the studio of Vatican Radio.

Ours was a big car, hired by a Texan prelate, but it cut small ice with the Roman police. We had to wait, prelate and all, while the eight Little Sisters of the Holy Sepulcher drove out in their Austin. They were demure and somber, probably examining their consciences. There was no sign of exultation on their Italian faces as they left all of us, cardinals, bishops, Texan theologians, behind.

We overtook them at the turning by the Columbus Hotel. The Sisters all turned their heads to the left and dipped their eyes in unison before our purple, but Reverend Mother, sitting next to Sister driver, gazed straight ahead.

Once we had passed, I could see through the driving mirror that the Little Sisters had no intention of being left in second place. Examination of conscience over for the moment, they were leaning forward to egg Sister chauffeur on. Their horn had a peremptory note about it, though the arrangement of its tootles fitted the midday Angelus. The Sisters turned their heads to the right and dropped their eyes in respect as they passed us.

The policeman at the junction, poised aloft in his precarious pulpit, raised his arm to check our flight. Our Texan driver slowed down just as he would have done in Dallas, unless he wanted a bullet through his chest. The Little Sisters of the Holy Sepulcher also slowed for a moment and, out of modesty, while our cars were level, dipped their eyes while looking straight ahead.

I think that Sister chauffeur meant to stop but Reverend Mother said something to her, and in a spirit of complete and blind obedience she zoomed ahead. My American friend, who knew Italian, swore that he heard the words, "Step on it, Sister!" They drew across the line of traffic, swerved right and left to miss the policeman, and vanished.

The policeman blew his whistle, abandoned his pulpit and the traffic, and stalked majestically to our Texan car. In a few choice phrases and with invocations to our Lady, St. Joseph, Fanfani, and Togliatti, he told us, as far as I could gather, what he would like to do to our necks.

"Say," said my Texan friend with dignity, "what about those Sisters?"

"Ah, where would we be without them?" asked the policeman.

Oodles of Noodles in Hong Kong

ê๛

BY ELWOOD D. BAUMANN

The American people meant well, of course, but the fifty-two million pounds of milk powder, cornmeal, and wheat flour shipped annually to Hong Kong did little to alleviate the suffering of the starving Chinese.

Many of the people lived in the streets and on rooftops. They were not familiar with milk powder or cornmeal. The flour was good, but most of the refugees had no stoves, mixing bowls, or baking pans.

They were grateful but bewildered. Several sampled mouthfuls of cornmeal or milk powder and found them unpalatable. What good was food if you couldn't eat it?

The more sourceful ones soon learned that the black market would give them a cup of rice or a few cents for their food packages. It wasn't much, but it was far better than nothing at all. Before long warehouses of local merchants were stacked high with food parcels marked "A Gift from the People of the United States."

Msgr. John Romaniello, M.M., director of Catholic Relief Services in Hong Kong, was distressed. Good food was being wasted while brave people starved and unscrupulous merchants grew wealthy. Day after day he wandered through the huge refugee resettlement areas searching for a solution to the problem. He couldn't condemn the people for selling their gifts on the black market. They simply did not know how to cook American foods.

One day he watched a skinny little Chinese girl trudging along with a bag of American flour clutched in her arms. He followed her and saw her enter a shop and hand the bag to a man. A moment later she emerged, carrying a much smaller parcel.

"What did you do with your flour?" he asked.

"Oh, I traded it off for a bag of noodles," the girl answered him proudly.

Noodles! Could this be the answer? The Chinese people like noodles and noddles are both filling and nutritious. "If I can make noodles," thought Monsignor Romaniello, "I can stop this shameful waste of good food and defeat the black marketeers at the same time."

Excitedly he rushed over to his friend Father Howard Trube, who had a reputation as an amateur cook. "Is it possible to make noodles from cornmeal, milk powder, and wheat flour?" he asked.

"Oh, yes, certainly," Father Trube assured him.

"How?"

"I don't know how. I just know it can be done. Leave it to me."

Knowing now that he had all the necessary ingredients for making noodles, Monsignor Romaniello called on Father Michael McKeirnan, director of a Hong Kong mission school, and informed him of his plan.

"It's a fine idea, I'm sure, John," agreed Father McKeirnan, "but just how do I fit into the scheme of things?"

"I want to use your school for a factory."

Accustomed to the monsignor's bursts of enthusiasm for any new idea, Father McKeirnan laughed. "So you want me to turn out the children and start turning out noodles. Is that it?"

"No, no, no! The children can stay. We only want to use some of the space behind the school for our factory," explained Monsignor Romaniello.

"I suppose, then, that you will fill the factory with great clanking macines that will drown out the drone of my voice when I'm lecturing," Father McKeirnan teased.

Machines? Why, of course, you had to have machines to make noodles. The monsignor had never seen a noodle-making machine, but he knew that there had to be such machines in Hong Kong. With Father McKeirnan in tow, he walked for hours through the congested streets looking for a noodle factory.

Late that afternoon they passed a hut where a Chinese workman was laboriously cranking the handle of a noodle-making machine. The two priests stood in the doorway and stared unabashedly. They watched the man put a mixture of flour and water into a hopper. When he turned a crank the ingredients were forced through a slit in the bottom, coming out in a wide, thin sheet. A series of knives divided the sheet into long strings, which were cut into three-foot lengths. The final step was to take them out into the sun and hang them over a clothesline to dry.

"How many pounds of noodles can you make in a day?" asked the monsignor, entering the hut.

"On a sunny day I can make about fifty pounds," replied the workman. "During rainy weather I'm nearly out of business because I can't get the noodles dry, and wet noodles get moldy."

It was obvious that a machine that made only fifty pounds of noodles a day was not going to be the answer to their problem.

But this was an antiquated, hand-run machine. Perhaps it would be possible to improve the design and power it with a motor.

Day after day Monsignor Romaniello and Father McKeirnan studied the machine while the old Chinese cranked out noodles. Neither of the priests had any mechanical training, but that slight handicap didn't deter them. They made and discarded page after page of drawings. The proprietor laughingly shook his head at their persistent questions and gently admonished them for nibbling at his noodles while they worked.

After a month of study they had what they considered a workable design. The manager of the Yoe On Hong Ironworks assured them that the machine was practical and agreed to build the first one at cost. Another hurdle had been overcome.

Meanwhile Father Trube was having problems of his own. The wheat flour, cornmeal, and milk powder refused to hold together. "I make the most beautiful noodle you've ever seen and then it crumbles into bits the minute it's dry," he complained to Father Romaniello.

It was not until the first noodle machine had been completed and six weeks of frustrating experimentation has passed that Father Trube found the right formula: 5% milk powder, 20% cornmeal, and 75% wheat flour.

He immediately informed the monsignor and the two men met at the factory behind Father McKeirnan's school. They started the electric motor on the noodle machine and put ten pounds of the mixture into the hopper. Out of the machine came soft, pliable sheets of dough which the knives sliced into long strings of perfect noodles. The priests hung the noodles on the clothesline and waited impatiently for the dough to dry.

Monsignor Romaniello broke the strings into twelve-inch lengths. They snapped cleanly and evenly. Clutching noodles in both hands, he pranced joyously around the machine, singing, "Noodles! I'm in the noodle business!"

One major hurdle still remained: money. Monsignor Romaniello began soliciting funds for his noodle operation from everyone he met. Tourists, businessmen, sailors, charitable organizations, and Hong Kong government officials all came to know the exuberant priest. Visitors to his office in the Man Yee Building were immediately prevailed upon to buy a copy of his book *Bird of Sorrow.* "It costs only two and a half Hong Kong dollars and that will buy a lot of noodles," he would say.

(*Bird of Sorrow* is the moving story of the communist occupation of Dragon Town, Kwangsi Province, in South China, where Father Romaniello served for twenty-two years before being expelled by the Red army. The book is published by the Noodle Press and is dedicated to "Millions of Noodles for Millions of Refugees.")

By October, 1957, the monsignor was producing five hundred pounds of noodles a day. They were packed in five-pound bags marked in English and Chinese, "Donated by the People of the United States." Assistants went to the refugee resettlement areas each morning and handed out white cards to one hundred people. In the afternoon the cards could be exchanged for bags of noodles.

"It was really rough at first," Monsignor Romaniello recalls. "The people understood that we couldn't feed them all every day. The one hundred with the white cards were always afraid that we would run out of noodles before we got to them, so they mobbed us.

"Remember that these people were starving. The Chinese are the most dignified in the world, but it is hard to maintain standards of dignity and courtesy when you are starving and somebody is handing out food parcels."

Wise to the ways of the Chinese he loves so much, the monsignor insists that each recipient thank him for the food. He insists, too, that each accept his package with both hands.

"That way," he explains, "they feel that it is a gift from their friends and not a mere handout."

"Romy's noodles," as they came to be called, were an instant success. Easy to cook and pleasant to eat, they were a great blessing for the refugees who worked long hours and lived in close quarters with little or no cooking space.

"You see, Father," a little refugee girl told the monsignor, "I'm the oldest child, so I have to take care of my brothers and sisters while my parents are working. The children have to be fed every evening and when I have noodles it's easy for me. I just boil them until they're cooked and then put them in rice bowls, and we have a wonderful meal."

"We hated having to sell our food packages on the black market," another refugee told him, "but we live on the sidewalk and we didn't know what to do with those strange American foods."

The one hundred refugees who received noodles every day were only a tiny fraction of the hungry people in Hong Kong. The city was already swollen with a million fugitives from Red China. They were still coming at the rate of 100,000 a year. Monsignor Romaniello knew that these resourceful, hard-working people would in time find ways of earning livings if they could survive the first few months. He vowed then that he would step up his efforts until he was distributing noodles to ten thousand refugees every day.

He persuaded the Hong Kong city government to give him land for factory sites and arranged to have six factories financed through the United States refugee program. Wealthy Chinese donated funds for machines; the Yoe On Hong Ironworks offered its facilities for making even larger machines. As the monsignor dashed about on his labor of love, he happily sang *The Noodle Song* (music and lyrics by John Romaniello). On the rare occasions when he took time off from his duties, he went out to the golf course and played for ten pounds of noodles a hole. . . .

I went with Monsignor Romaniello one cool afternoon in November, 1960, to the sordid Shaukiwan district to distribute noodles. Thousands of huts dotted the hillsides; sheds leaned against buildings in narrow lanes. "Home" meant any space large enough for sleeping room and every corner was occupied. Six hundred people with white cards were lined up in an alley. "Here comes the noodle priest!" children shouted happily when he arrived.

I helped distribute food parcels and was deeply moved to see the hungry but proud people reach out eagerly for their five-pound bags. "That gentleman," Monsignor Romaniello said at one point, nodding toward a gray-haired patriarch, "used to be a millionaire businessman in Canton. Today he has to stand in food lines."

Less than an hour before, I had disgustedly thrown down a copy of the *Wall Street Journal* because the market was off for the third consecutive day.

Now I found myself handing out parcels of food to hungry men who had known much better days. I suddenly felt humble and ashamed. Soon I would be returning to my large, comfortable room in the Foreign Correspondents' club; many of these people would return to pieces of canvas on the sidewalk. For the first time in many long months I stopped to count my blessings.

IT'S THE THOUGHT THAT COUNTS

When Father Robert J. Ledogar was asked by friends what gift he would like for his ordination, he suggested a pair of oil stocks, the small vessels in which sacramental oils are kept.

He was speechless when the gift arrived—two shares of Standard Oil of New Jersey.

Charles Chick Govin.

HO, HO, HO

The Maryknoll Sisters had sent one of their finest to give a talk on vocations to our grade-school girls. She was full of wit and humor. Her audience was captivated by her radiant happiness.

One mother reported that when her little girl came home from school, she threw open the door and announced, "Mommy, when I grow up I'm going to be a Merry Old Nun."

John R. Bourque.

THAT SUIT AND COLLAR

We live close to the rectory and our three-year-old Kathy makes frequent visits to the monsignor and his assistant. Not long ago the assistant was transferred and a new young priest came to take his place. We wondered how this decision of the bishop's would rest with Kathy, but we said nothing to her about it.

Came a day when she went over for her usual call. She came back in just a few minutes in a state of high excitement. "Mother!" she shouted, "There's a strange man over there and he's got on Father's clothes!"

Mrs. Wayne Crawford.

A QUESTION OF IDENTITY

When I was a newly ordained priest, I went out to help in a certain parish over Holy Week. The pastor was a tough character who seemed never to have a kind word for me during the entire week. He did, however, have a dog on whom he lavished all his affection.

Easter Sunday evening the pastor offered to drive me home. We three got into his car, with the dog going to sleep on the floor of the back seat, and myself riding next to the pastor up front. We stopped to get gas and while the attendant filled the tank and wiped the windshield, Father paced restlessly up and down outside.

Then the attendant made a move to wipe the side windows. Father waved him off, shouting, "Don't bother with those. That fool inside will just slobber all over them anyhow!" I tried to get the dog to sit up and take a bow, but he was too smart to move.

Joseph T. McGloin, S.J., in the Twin Citian.

ONE MEETS SUCH INTERESTING PEOPLE!

I was alone and stranded in London, the war-torn and bomb-weary London of 1946. My ultimate destination was our Marist mother house in Italy, but my American superior had granted me permission to go there in this leisurely fashion, with stop-offs in Ireland, England, and France. Through some mixup the Brother who was to meet me in London had failed to appear, and I had resigned myself to a bench in the waiting room for the night.

By great good luck I spied three touring Yanks, whose open-front collars identified them as La Salle Brothers. I explained my predicament, asking if they knew of any hotels that might have a room. No, they knew of none, but they themselves had managed to put up at a small boardinghouse in Bayswater. Perhaps the landlady could find room for one more.

The owners turned out to be a splendid Italian couple whose

daughter attended a Marist school. They ousted the son of the house from his room to take me in, and from this headquarters I spent several pleasant days visiting the sights of London.

When I was due to leave for Paris, the landlady asked me to deliver a package. I was happy to oblige, so she wrapped up several chocolate bars and addressed the parcel to a priest in Paris, explaining that he was an old family friend.

In Paris I took a cab to the address on the package. It turned out to be an imposing residence on the Seine. I hesitated. This could hardly be the home of an Italian priest. But I rang the bell and soon found myself ushered into the presence of Archbishop Roncalli, then papal nuncio to France!

Archbishop Roncalli recalled at once the friends of his boyhood in Italy. No gift of precious jewels was ever more enthusiastically received than the humble offering I presented. Well do I recall the warm embrace and accolade, after the manner of Latins, that he gave me. Hearing of my difficulties in London, he insisted that I be his house guest during my stay in Paris. This invitation I regretfully declined; I was already installed with the Marist Brothers of the city. Need I add that later developments have magnified my regret?

Brother John Lawrence O'Shea, f.m.s.

CONFIRMED BEATLES

The priest was instructing a confirmation class. "Be certain, girls, that your hair style leaves the forehead open so the bishop can mark it with holy chrism." Then, as an afterthought, he added, "I guess that goes for the boys, too."

Mrs. Dean Pierce.

JOHN AND LEO

Comment of Pope John XXIII, when shown the design for his papal coat of arms: "Please don't make my lion look so cross."

James B. Simpson.

THE ANNUAL GREETINGS

Last Easter our elderly pastor, looking over the unusually large congregation, worked us up with this announcement: "Dearest brethren, I realize that I will not see many of you again until next Easter, so permit me to take this opportunity to wish all of you a merry Christmas and a happy New Year!"

Raymond J. Ross.

SORRY, WRONG NUMBER

Sister Mary Ignatia, audio-visual director of the College of St. Catherine in St. Paul, Minnesota, needed to get the rating on a certain movie film. She dialed what she thought was the Legion of Decency number and an unfamiliar voice answered the phone. "Hello," she said. "Is this the Legion of Decency?"

"No," the voice replied. "But you have the next thing to it. This is the Pure Oil Company."

S.M.I.

CONFUSION OF TONGUES

The superior of the Columban Fathers at Ba, Fiji Islands, Patrick J. Kelly, is an Irishman from County Galway. He offered his first Mass one Sunday at Lautoka, the chief town of Fiji's largest island, Viti Levu, in English. His second Mass at Vitogo, five miles distant, was offered in Fijian. His third Mass, at an Indian cane farmers' settlement called Lovo, was offered in Hindi. At other places, the vernacular is Rotuman.

Columban Mission News Release.

HERE'S YOUR HAT

Louise rushed home from second grade and requested an advance on her allowance.

"What for?" I asked.

"A real big thing, Mom," Louise explained. "Father Beaver is leaving Assumption and the kids want to give him a little momentum."

Margie Miller.

DELAYED ACTION

At a U.N. gathering actress Shelley Winters and a dignified nun walked up to sign the guest register at the same time. Miss Winters, anxious to get the ceremony over with, didn't know she had stepped directly in front of the nun until her companion cautioned her, "Wait till the nun signs, Shelley."

Mrs. H. Priday.

VALLEY OF DEATH

Father Gustave Weigel, who briefed the observers of non-Catholic churches during the Council, died in 1964. Earlier he had two operations for cancer while at Woodstock College and became so ill that a grave in the Woodstock cemetery was opened for his body. Meanwhile another Jesuit priest died and the rector asked Father Weigel if he would yield his grave to him. His answer: "The proposition seems very unfair to me, but, oh well, since he is an old friend, he can have it."

Juan Ochagavia in Woodstock Letters.

ECUMENICAL SOFTBALL

A softball team made up of priests from the Ashtabula, Ohio, area was defeated 12–7 by a team of ministers. The seven-inning game was umpired by a rabbi.

The only discordant note was the priests' use of a seminarian to round out their squad. The ministers complained about the unfair use of a "farm team" player.

NCWC.

CHANGING TIMES

Sister Maria Del Rey, the former newspaperwoman-turned-nun, is well known for her best-selling books such as *Safari by Jet.* Recently she started an advanced journalism course at Columbia University, New York City. Her professor gave her an assignment to get an offbeat, human-interest story at the Marriage License Bureau.

She took the subway downtown, found the bureau, and walked up to the license counter. She noticed that everyone had stopped work and was staring at her in amazement. Finally, a young man approached her and when she told him what she was looking for, he blurted out a fine brogue, "Glory be to God, Sister! When I saw you walk in I says to myself, 'They're going too far with this Ecumenical Council!' "

St. Paul Cenacle Star.

FACE TO FACE

"Often when near sleep I happen to think of some serious problem and I may say to myself, 'I must speak to the Pope about this.' And then, completely awake, I remember that I *am* Pope!" The speaker was Pope John XXIII.

The New York Times.

FLIGHTS OF FANCY

Black and white bouquet of nuns—*Janet Gillespie.*
Monsignor had forty-eight pounds that hadn't been ordained—

M. K. Koestler.

III ARTS AND LETTERS

Illustration from *Mr. Spooner and Mrs. Malaprop*

Portrait of a Pope

ह्≫

BY BERNARD GODWIN

To paint the portrait of a Pope is always a great honor; to paint the first portrait from life of Pope John XXIII was also a great responsibility.

Before leaving New York I examined every available photograph. Later, in Rome, Metro-Goldwyn-Mayer ran off for me newsreels featuring the Pope. I examined each frame on a still machine. By that time I thought that I had all the necessary information on Pope John's features, body structure, and expression. It would not be long, however, before I discovered that no image made by mechanical means captures his true personality.

The Pope is not photogenic and doesn't like to have his picture taken. Moreover, a split-second exposure cannot record the ever changing expressions that play over his face. The basic characterization of the Holy Father, one of gentle benevolence accompanied by the shadow of a smile and a twinkle in the eyes, can be caught only on canvas.

Through the kind offices of Archbishop Martin J. O'Connor, rector of the North American College in Rome, I was privileged to have a seat very close to the papal throne on Christmas day, 1958. Now for the first time I saw His Holiness at close range.

His gaze was directed upward—sensitive, serious, almost anxious, as he prepared to officiate at Mass. The head was large and oval; the hands, strong and sensitive; the body, round and slightly under medium height.

His Holiness mounted the ten steps to the altar with surprising agility. In a strong, melodious voice he intoned the first prayers. For forty minutes he conducted each action with vigor. As the Mass came to an end he descended from the altar. His countenance had about it a unique spiritual quality, as though the Lord had looked upon him and suffused his face with a special glory. I was never to see exactly the same expression on the Pope's face again.

Not long after, I received my invitation to a private audience. During my long career as a portrait painter of men such as Sir Alexander Fleming, Prof. Albert Einstein, Gen. George C. Marshall, Dr. Jonas Salk, and others, the prospect of confronting a famous subject never caused me any emotional upset. But I must admit that as I awaited the Pope the thought of meeting him had me quaking in my boots.

One last look at my watch told me that the time was at hand. Swiftly through the door came a short, rotund man dressed in flowing white robes. His warm smile quickly relieved all my pent-up anxieties.

The papal secretary formally introduced me to the Holy Father. I knelt but arose at his gesture. We exchanged amenities and, for what seemed a full minute, we looked into each other's eyes. Then he smiled and directed me toward the throne.

Once again here was a different personality. Now the Pope was calm, relaxed, and jovial. However, I did detect an inquiring note, as if he wondered what kind of an ordeal lay ahead as he sat for his first portrait as Pope.

I had to touch the Pope to show how he was to sit. In my concentration I had forgotten the tradition: nobody touches the Pope! Every time I did so, I heard muffled gasps from his secretary. The Holy Father heard these reactions, but he smiled broadly.

I was reminded at that moment of a story going the rounds in Rome. The Holy Father, so the tale went, walked one day into the Vatican garage. He saw a small boy watching with great interest the mechanics who were overhauling one of the papal cars.

The Pope loves children. "What is your name?" he asked the fascinated boy. "My name is Cardinal," the lad replied, barely looking up and then bending again to watch the work. Pope John looked at him with some amusement. "Ah! yes," he said, "I had forgotten. You must be one of the new cardinals I appointed a few weeks ago."

Remembering that story helped me to relax. The dimensions of the Pope's head, I found, are slightly larger than average. I observed the light brown eyes, a nose that is long and curved at the end, the generous mouth. It is the Pope's mouth which displays changes of emotion from solemn seriousness to the whimsy of a gentle smile.

The skin texture of his face is youthfully smooth and has the tone of porcelain. Except for a few shallow wrinkles on his forehead the Holy Father appears much younger than his seventy-eight years. His temples are covered with silky, steel-gray hair.

The Pope's hands are extremely interesting to an artist. They are large and powerful, yet well shaped and sensitive. I asked the Holy Father to grasp my hand so that I might feel the strength of his grip. The pressure was considerable.

Finally I stepped back to my easel and began to sketch in detail. The overall impression of his frame is one of solidity. I had no doubt that before me was a man majestic and noble, of great wisdom and kindliness.

After posing for some time, Pope John became restless and beads of perspiration formed on his brow. The chamber was quite warm and his woolen robes looked extremely uncomfortable. "Now I understand how the saints felt when they were burned at the stake," he remarked.

I proposed a break in the sitting so that His Holiness could get some rest. He refused. "I must not interrupt the artist's work. Please continue."

A few minutes later, when I was painting the mouth, an amusing incident took place. To catch the color of his lips I asked my sitter to moisten them. Since I found difficulty in explaining this in French, our only mutual language, I tried to roll my tongue over my lips. I was startled to hear instead that I was making a quacking sound. At first, I think, the Holy Father thought that I was imitating a duck or trying to be funny. When he finally understood, we both had a hearty laugh.

Soon the sitting was over. I approached the throne and chatted for a few minutes with His Holiness. We spoke of America and the President. I asked the Pope if he would ever visit the United States.

"I would like to visit your country," he said, "but I do not have the time." A few more words were exchanged. I then knelt and said farewell. With a smile Pope John rose from his throne, fingered his cross with his right hand, and left the room just as swiftly as he had entered.

The Wistful World
of Brother Juniper

ε๖

BY THEODORE IRWIN

Almost any afternoon an ascetic-looking priest in a monastic robe may be seen strolling through the Boston suburb of Brookline, seemingly lost in meditation. Every once in a while he pauses, breaks into a grin, then digs into his pocket for a pencil stub and a pad. The memo made, he walks on.

His scrawls are ideas for a cartoon series featuring a puckish, roly-poly friar called Brother Juniper, who appears in 102 newspapers in the United States and thirteen foreign countries. Brother Juniper's creator, Father Justin McCarthy, O.F.M., has an audience of fifteen million.

In less than three years the cartoon's popularity has grown phenomenally. Gift shops are enjoying brisk sales of sixty different Brother Juniper ceramic items, such as figurines, plates, cups and saucers, planters, clocks, and children's lamps. Three Juniper cartoon books have hit the million-copy mark. Brother

Juniper appeared on TV last year as a symbol of Brotherhood Week.

Brother Juniper fans consider their favorite a saintly Sad Sack in sackcloth. Father McCarthy, who signs his cartoons "Fr. Mac," actually modeled him after a thirteenth-century friar. Holy without suspecting it, Juniper saves souls with an appealingly mischievous personality. A devoted fan, FBI chief J. Edgar Hoover, once remarked: "I have a hard time realizing that Brother Juniper is not actually a real person."

Brother Juniper's blithe expression bears a striking resemblance to that of his creator. Sometimes persons who meet the forty-two-year-old Father McCarthy blurt out, "Why, *you* are Brother Juniper!" Unlike the cherubic Juniper, however, he is five feet, eight inches tall, wears glasses, and has an athletic physique. But the twinkle in his eye is undeniably that of his heavenly minded jester.

"Juniper," he admits, "is an extension of myself—or vice versa."

Father McCarthy lives with seven other priests at St. Francis Friary in Brookline. His spacious, sparsely furnished room is dominated by three large work tables. A rickety lamp, too low for his drawing board, has to rest on a thick volume of Shakespeare.

"The Bard," he says deadpan, "is indispensable to my work."

Like the other priests, he offers Mass daily, hears Confessions, preaches, and holds himself available for counseling. In the afternoon he takes a three-mile hike or keeps circling the secluded garden at the rear of the friary, thinking up his gags. After supper he reworks and sharpens them before doing his rough sketches.

He draws with a swift left hand—"the fastest draw in the East," he claims. Each week he illustrates twenty gags, of which six must be good enough for publication.

All his rough cartoons are reviewed by a "censorship board" composed of Father Gerard Fitzsimmons (his superior at the friary) and Msgr. Francis Lally, editor of the Boston *Pilot*, the diocesan newspaper. Father McCarthy, who worries that he may unintentionally wound someone's feelings, insists that he finds this censorship helpful. "I want my cartoons to be clean as a hound's tooth, to be wholly unobjectionable to anyone," he says. "My board picks the funniest, those with the broadest appeal."

The priest then passes on his approved roughs to Len Reno, a professional cartoonist who inks them into finished form.

His inspiration often comes from acute observation of human frailties as well as from his wide reading. His favorite humorists are England's A. P. Herbert, Canada's Stephen Leacock, America's Damon Runyon, and the famous Jewish comedian Menasha Skulnik.

As a youngster Justin McCarthy started drawing cartoons with a box of kindergarten crayons. By twelve he had a collection of rejection slips from *The New Yorker*. At Boston college he did some cartooning for football programs and the college weekly.

At the end of his sophomore year, when he was twenty, he decided to become a Franciscan priest. "The life and spirit of Saint Francis," he recalls, "appealed strongly to me. He had a popular approach, preaching the love of God to the common man simply and directly."

Franciscans take a vow of poverty. Father McCarthy's father was a prosperous engineer-architect and the young man had been brought up in what he calls a very comfortable environment. Yet poverty didn't faze him. "Instead of being burdened with all the encumbrances of civilization," he says, "I wanted to go back to the simplicity of the original Gospel as Saint Francis did." He was ordained in 1944.

His effervescent sense of humor soon bubbled to the surface through his yen for cartooning. During the Second World War a newsletter was sent to the many Franciscan chaplains scattered throughout the world. On a page of cartoons, his Friar Sad Sack became the progenitor of Brother Juniper.

About ten years ago Father McCarthy developed a serious throat condition that made him fear he would lose his voice.

Since he realized that a priest without a voice wouldn't be able to preach, he sought another means of communication.

"Following my natural bent," he says, "and hooking it up to the Franciscan tradition of appealing to the masses in a popular manner, I hit upon the cartoon as my medium."

Fortunately his throat trouble cleared up after three years. He is now able to accept a stream of public-speaking engagements.

As art director of *Friar*, a national Franciscan magazine, he introduced several cartoon features. His work impressed an author's agent, Jules Fields, who sold the idea of a religious cartoon to Harold H. Anderson, editor of Publishers Syndicate, of Chicago. "It was a case of a Catholic cartoonist being sold by a Jewish agent to a Methodist editor," Father McCarthy observes.

Before he could launch Juniper he had to clear the cartoon with his provincial, the Very Reverend Celsus R. Wheeler, O.F.M., and Boston Archbishop Richard Cushing. Juniper made his first appearance on December 9, 1957, and ever since has been brightening the day for readers of the Los Angeles *Times*, the Chicago *Daily News*, the New York *Mirror*, and other newspapers.

Juniper has brought financial rewards: $30,000 a year from syndication alone. Father McCarthy, sworn to poverty, doesn't accept a dime. The money is used chiefly to help Franciscan seminary students.

Juniper is not a pure figment of Father McCarthy's imagination. The character is based on a real Brother Juniper, called "the holy clown of the Franciscan Order," who lived during the early thirteenth century. Father McCarthy had read legends about him in the *Fioretti*, a classic collection of legends about St. Francis and his companions. In one story the kindly little friar lets some poor thieves take the robe off his back so that they won't go away empty-handed.

Traditionally Juniper was a bumbling benefactor who was always tripping over his feet. No matter how rudely he was treated, he always bounced back with a smile. As Father McCarthy has conceived his twentieth-century Juniper, he is "one part Friar Tuck, two parts Victor Moore, three parts George Bungle, four parts Everyman, a pinch of Pogo, and a *soupçon* of Bishop Sheen."

Through his little goodwill envoy, Father McCarthy tries to get in a gentle message. "As long as he is making people happy, Brother Juniper is fulfilling his destiny and mine, too," he says.

His own favorite Juniper cartoon shows a fence on which youngsters have written, "Debbie Loves Pete," "Andy loves Betty," and similar sentiments. But Juniper letters in his own endearment: "LOVE THY NEIGHBOR." Another of his pet cartoons has Juniper in a pulpit announcing to the congregation: "But first, a message from Our Sponsor."

The Reverend Everett R. Clinchy, past president of the National Conference of Christians and Jews, has given the cartoon his "wholehearted endorsement." A Congregationalist minister in Evanston, Illinois, once wrote that Juniper's "warm and tender humor is part of the universal language."

Among those who have voiced any adverse criticism was one reader who didn't like to see Juniper smoking a cigar. Occasionally Father McCarthy has goofed. He may or may not have when he showed Juniper milking a cow, with a caption reading,

"How about one for the road?" A barrage of letters and phone calls reminded him that "you never milk a cow from the left side." For a while after that he confined Juniper to urban chores.

Another cartoon had the little friar playing a piccolo with a bird perched on the instrument and Juniper imploring it to "get your foot off B-flat!" Again a flood of letters, mostly from children, informed him that he had misplaced his B-flat.

Father McCarthy is an avid Baltimore Colt football fan and also takes in an occasional big-league baseball game. A spare-time sculptor, he did a figure of Christ writing in the sand which won second prize several years ago in the New England Art Festival. In the summer, when he serves his Order at Wareham, Massachusetts, he often teaches children how to swim.

He plays softball in Brookline streets with the boys. Many Juniper cartoons show the merry friar in baseball situations. One showed a couple of small fry announcing to an astonished monk, "Brother Juniper said we could keep our bats in your belfry."

Most of the Brookline children he plays with are Jewish, a fact which may account for one cartoon in which Juniper stands on the shoulders of a colleague to peer over his monastery wall and call out to a passerby, "Happy Hanukkah, Mrs. Goldberg!"

Father McCarthy thinks his brand of humor has wide appeal because of the public's identification with the undefeated under-dog. "People recognize that whatever happens to Brother Juniper could happen to them," he says. "Perhaps he helps teach us that there should be no place for pride on earth.

"If Brother Juniper tickles the funny bone—well, that's not too far from the heart; and from there it's only a hop, skip, and jump to the soul."

O'Malley and the Little Nuns

ह≫

BY MARY DANA RODRIGUEZ

Two nuns were walking along a Carmel, California, street recently. A passerby stopped them. "You're Bill O'Malley's nuns—Sisters Maureen and Colleen," he said happily. "I'd know you anywhere."

It wasn't the first time such an identification had been made. O'Malleys nuns are two lovable little figures with a knack for getting in and out of unexpected situations. Since the artist who draws them lives and works in Carmel, any Sister in the community is suspect.

Is there actually a Sister Maureen and a Sister Colleen? "That question has been put to me hundreds of times," says artist Bill O'Malley. "The answer is No. They're a composite of all the Sisters I've ever known.

"Some of my earliest and pleasantest memories are of nuns and more nuns," he continues. "In Oakland, California, where I grew up, we had Sisters teaching at Saint Joseph and at Sacred Heart schools. All the kids liked them. They were strict but fair and always managed to keep a sense of humor."

79

Early in his cartooning career, when some religious magazine asked him for contributions, Bill recalled his school days and dreamed up Sister Maureen and Sister Colleen. They were an instant hit. Today a devoted audience snaps up every collection of O'Malley's cartoons the minute they are published.

His books receive similar acclaim abroad. Sometimes the nuns are renamed. In West Germany, for example, they become Sister Monika and Sister Veronika.

The basic reason for their popularity was summed up in a recent column by Gary Bunson, book reviewer of the San Francisco *Chronicle*. He wrote : "Bill O'Malley's cartoons, the best in the religious field, are proof that real humor can be generated without offense."

Bill started cartooning when he was on the staff of the now defunct Oakland *Post Inquirer*. He had received his formal art education at Oakland's California Arts and Crafts School after graduation from Technical High.

"I had quite a schedule those days," O'Malley recalls. "After school I would caddy. Then, when the sun went down, I'd hang around the newspaper office. After graduation it seemed the natural thing for the *Post Inquirer* to put me to work. And since I had studied art and liked golfing, it was still more natural for me to become a sports cartoonist."

Then Bill met a petite, pretty girl from Norway named Ada and fell in love. He knew that if he was going to get married, he would have to supplement his income. The solution: free-lance work—and O'Malley's Nuns.

Bill and Ada were married in 1926 in St. Leo's Church in Oakland. Ada, a convert, is a devoted rooter for Sisters Colleen and Maureen. "I feel so proud when I see Bill's pocket books on a store rack," she says.

The O'Malleys moved to Carmel by degrees. They left Oakland to live across the bay in San Francisco when Bill went to work in the art department of the San Francisco *Call-Bulletin,* now the *News-Bulletin.* Then, in 1946, they progressed to Carmel.

"We used to spend all our vacations and many a weekend in Carmel," explains Bill. "In fact, I think we have stayed in practically every room in the La Playa Hotel. We finally decided we'd give up visiting and move here."

The O'Malleys now live a few blocks from the La Playa in a typical Carmel home. It is a small, picturesque house, with a redwood gate, a light blue garage door, and, in its beautifully wood-paneled living room, a lavender ceiling.

"That's about par for Carmel," Bill claims. "No street lights, no house numbers, no mail delivery, but lots of quaintness. We love it."

In 1951, after Bill had drawn enough of his *Two Little Nuns* cartoons to compile a book, he and his publishers found themselves with a best seller on their hands.

"I think every nun in America got at least five copies for Christmas," says Bill. "People love to give them as gifts to nuns and priests."

Since then Bill has had two more books about the innocent antics of his Sisters. The second is called *O'Malley's Nuns;* the third, *More O'Malley's Nuns.*

He gets baskets of fan letters, many of which begin, "I read your cartoons religiously." The mail he likes best is from children. He especially treasures an uphill-printed note from a small girl who stated only, "I love you. I love your nuns."

It is easy to like Bill O'Malley. He is one of the most popular members of the Carmel artists' colony.

"When we first moved here, it would take Bill only ten minutes to go down to the post office and get our mail. But now when he goes there, I'm lucky if he gets back in an hour and a half," says Mrs. O'Malley. "It's the favorite meeting place of the community and Bill knows everybody and everybody knows him."

When the O'Malleys travel, it isn't just around the corner. They love cruises, long ones. "We're always either just coming from a cruise or planning another one, it seems," says Bill. "We usually go by freighter."

In deference to Ada's Norwegian background (she's from Hammerfest, the most northerly city in the world) they generally choose Norwegian freighters. "That's because it's the only way I get to speak Norwegian and enjoy my native dishes," she explains. "Bill likes Scandinavian cooking aboard ship, but at home, no."

There is no respite for artist O'Malley on these trips. Even before the ship leaves the dock in San Francisco, he has his collapsible easel set up and is hard at work.

"His working hours are no different when we are supposedly on vacation than when he is at home," sighs Mrs. O'Malley. "When he isn't eating or sleeping, he's drawing. Even in Papeete, Tahiti, our favorite port, Bill still keeps up a rigid working schedule."

Most people, particularly fellow cartoonists, are amazed at Bill's daily schedule. He is a fast worker, who can finish four to five drawings in an hour. Unlike most syndicated cartoonists, Bill does all his drawings and writes all his own gags. He is also his own agent, but Ada handles most of his business affairs.

"I also clean his studio," she adds, "though he claims he can't find anything unless it is completely messed up."

Although Bill is best known for his Little Nuns cartoons, he turns out another popular feature, the syndicated comic strip the *Reverend*. The strip features an amiable clergyman of an unspecified denomination.

As with the Little Nuns, there is a celestial tinge to the Reverend's humor. In one panel, for example, he is seen proudly accepting first prize at a county fair for his divinity fudge. The

Reverend got his start five years ago when Bill won second prize in a cartoon contest held by United Features Syndicate to develop new material.

Versatile Bill also has his signature on cartoon books covering a wide variety of subjects. The titles include: *Golf Fore Fun, Bon Bon Voyage, Blessed Event,* and *Feeling No Pain.*

His single cartoons have appeared in most leading magazines, including the *Saturday Evening Post* and *Gourmet.*

However, it is still his amusingly human conception of the Little Nuns that keeps Bill out front.

"I am supposed to be an authority on nuns," he says, "but there is one thing I am not sure of and keep forgetting to ask about. That is, how many pockets a Sister has in her habit."

Bill is his own censor. "I use my own yardstick of good taste," he says. "I am happy to report that I have never had any complaints from a religious Order. The letters I do get from nuns tell me how much they like my cartoons and even suggest comic situations."

The O'Malleys are parishioners of Carmel's beautiful Mission Basilica, built in the adobe Spanish style in a garden setting. The mission was founded in 1770 by Father Junipero Serra, who is buried there. In 1960 it was raised to the status of a basilica by Pope John.

Besides O'Malley, other established cartoonists who live in Carmel and its environs are Jimmy Hatlo, Gus Arriola, Frank O'Neal, Bob Barnes, Lee Holley, and the Pulitzer-Prize-winning political cartoonist Vaughn Shoemaker. The Carmel cartoonists get together often, with the O'Malleys in their midst.

"But not at large cocktail parties," Bill explains. "Ada and I decided long ago to give up attending big brawls. I know a number of cartoonists who claim they get some of their best ideas at parties. But with the sort of stuff I draw, a cocktail party is the last place I would get an inspiration."

The O'Malleys have no children, a fact that has not always

been apparent to new acquaintances or neighbors. Bill is the loudest rooter for Carmel's Little League. He and Ada often have the children of relatives or friends staying with them.

Not long ago one young lad who was spending the week with the O'Malleys came home and found the living room filled with sixteen black-and-white-robed Sisters from Fresno.

"He had never seen so many nuns in one place in his life and was terrified," says Bill, "but the Sisters soon charmed him into having lunch with them. I explained that things like that are bound to happen when you visit a fellow who draws nuns for a living. Basic research, you know—on both sides."

Little Moe

ॐ

BY HAROLD HELFER

If you were asked, you might say that the most popular comic strip in the world is Blondie. Or Beetle Bailey. Or maybe Pogo. Or Li'l Abner. Or Orphan Annie.

You'd be wrong. The most widely spread and undoubtedly most widely read comic-strip creation is Little Moe. Moe is a winsome, bedraggled little character who is almost completely overwhelmed by austere and inhuman forces about him but somehow manages to hang on. He appears in some five hundred newspapers in fifty-nine countries and is probably read by at least fifty million people.

Read is really not the right word. Many, many things happen to him and it is obvious that he can get quite soulful, but he never says anything. It's part of his charm that no matter how much he has to take it on the chin he never complains.

It wouldn't do him much good to squawk, anyhow. For the life and times of Little Moe is strictly behind the Iron Curtain. In simple and graphic eloquence he symbolizes existence at its most sterile and arbitrary, as it would be in an undemocratic, bureaucratic land.

Though Little Moe is drawn in this country by an American artist he has never appeared in a publication in the United States. Another thing that's unique about this rather beat-uplike but gritty little fellow is that he was created by the U.S. Government, probably the only comic-strip character ever to be hatched by Uncle Sam.

Little Moe is such a beguiling little fellow that it is hard to believe that he is a purely propaganda instrument. He is produced by the U.S. Information Agency for the sole purpose of bringing home the haplessness of people under dictatorial communism.

Some people think that this little urchin may be the most powerful propaganda blast that we have going for us abroad. Certain it is that he is appearing in newspapers and other publications in countries that would toss away any kind of heavy-handed propaganda tract. He appears right up against the cannons of communism, in Laos and Vietnam newspapers, for instance, where the nations aren't likely to go out of their way to incur the wrath of nearby belligerent communist forces. But Little Moe is such a winning fellow that it is hard to resist him. And once he has appeared in a newspaper, readers clamor for more of him.

But for all his waifish charm Little Moe always makes a point. In one strip, for instance, he digs his way to freedom out of a Siberian mine. In another he uses a Russian flagpole to vault over the communist wall into West Berlin. In another he raises a Russian-made umbrella and gets drenched by rain that pours through the holes in it—in fact, he keeps getting drenched by this umbrella even after the sun comes out. Then there's the one that shows him on a bleak, cold, and barren day—as all his days seem to be—finding a wall with a tree limb stuck against it. He draws flowers on the wall, at the twig ends, in an effort to brighten things up a little.

The total result of all this is to get the feeling that the workers' paradise the communists keep hammering-and-sickling about is not such a heavenly place, that life there is on the stark, drab, and downtrodden side. And, of course, this is the intent. Little Moe fans are supposed to get the idea that they'd just as soon not wind up behind the Iron Curtain.

While the point in any Little Moe strip is always made with disarming simplicity, it is nevertheless very tough to come by. Not only does everything have to be in pantomime because of the language barrier involved with something that appears in so many different countries; but even signs, such as "Detour" or "Keep Off the Grass," have to be avoided, and any symbols used have to be chosen with great care. For instance, a telephone booth would mean nothing to many quarters of the world; it might suggest an outhouse to many readers.

The artist, who signs these strips Rideo but whose real name is Everett Dee Fairchild, spends many a painstaking hour on the strips. An Oklahoman who grew up in Texas, he has the title of Chief of the Graphic Arts Section for the U.S. Information Agency, but his main job is getting out Little Moe.

"I can think of a lot of different dire situations to get Moe into," says artist Fairchild, "but I've got to get him out of them, too."

Little Moe is ten years old. The chances are that he isn't likely to become widely known among American readers, since Federal policy is against Government-produced features appearing in the country's commercial press. But he seems destined to become a permanent part of this nation's effort to "spread the word" around the world, at least as long as communism and the Iron Curtain exist as a major world threat.

Mr. Spooner
and
Mrs. Malaprop

ဇ&

BY EDWIN NEWMAN

We all make mistakes and sometimes the mistakes are more attractive than the correct version. When President Kennedy nominated Gen. Lyman Lemnitzer as the new United States and NATO commander in Europe, an NBC commentator referred to the general as "Lemon Lymnitzer."

"Lemon Lymnitzer" is a spoonerism, named for the British clergyman William Archibald Spooner (1844–1930). Canon Spooner might have been much happier if some theological distinction had attached to his name, but in history he will be the man who read to his congregation, "Now Rababbas was a bobber." He would say "blushing crow" when he meant crushing blow and he turned conquering kings into "kinquering congs."

In the days before television the classic among radio spooner-isms was Harry Von Zell's. He renamed a President of the United States "Hoobert Heever." Not quite spoonerisms, but related, were Graham MacNamee's advertising of "Texaco Fire Chief Gasoloon" and someone else's reference to "General Dwight Eisenhowever."

A splendid effort by an NBC commentator came during a report on the stock market. He wanted to say that blue-chip stocks had fallen but said instead "blue-chop sticks." I have myself rendered the Dow-Jones averages into the "Dough-Jowns."

Another radio correspondent reported that a member of Congress had described a certain diplomat as a "pushie cooker." Trinking dee and wearing piped strants, presumably.

Spoonerisms are not the only speech mistakes that can be funny. There is the malaprop, named for Mrs. Malaprop in Richard Brinsley Sheridan's eighteenth-century play *The Rivals*. Mrs. Malaprop describes somebody as "a progeny of learning." At one point she announces, "If I reprehend anything in this world, it is the use of my oracular tongue, and a nice derange-ment of epitaphs."

There was a commendable contribution in this field by a mayor of Chicago, who was certain that the city would rise to "new platitudes of achievement."

A malaprop usually proceeds from affectation, from an attempt to seem important by using grandiose words. It can lead you astray in the same way that mistaken foreign phrases can. I once ate in a restaurant that for some reason had its menu in French. Instead of calling something a tomato salad, which it was, it used the French, *salade de tomates*. Unfortunately it came out *salaud de tomates*. *Salaud* is a word the French apply to a very filthy person.

In the misuse of foreign words the spoken error is usually

89

more amusing than the written. I was once told by a New York businessman that the trouble with President de Gaulle was that he thought of himself as another Joan D. Arc, and that the trouble with the French people was that they had no spirit de corps. To quote someone else, this may have been the work of an *Asian provocateur*.

Here are some of the most intriguing errors I have heard. In conversation "multiple cirrhosis," a truly dread disease; "up-evils," something the Middle East was going through; "bonzana," what a colleague with a new contract was enjoying, according to his insurance agent. On radio: "operating at fervor pitch." On television: "beautified," which was how two Americans had been dealt with by the Vatican as a preliminary to possible sanctification; "anxious viggle," which turned out to be anxious vigil, and not, as might be thought, a description of the action of a nervous worm.

I lived for a while in London. A Foreign Office man of my acquaintance treasured a semispoonerism committed by an American aid official in Greece. The American, at the end of his assignment, was given a dinner by Greeks he had worked with. He knew no Greek; but it was thought that it would be pleasant if he could at any rate express his thanks in Greek. The word required was *Epharisto* and the American was told to remember it as though it were "F. Harry Stowe." When the time came, he rose grandly and said, "My friends, all I can say to you is Harry F. Stowe." Saying which, he sat down.

Learn with BOOK

ॐ

BY R. J. HEATHORN

A new aid to rapid—almost magical—learning has made its appearance. Indications are that if it catches on, all the electronic gadgets will be so much junk. The new device is known as Built-in Orderly Organized Knowledge. The makers generally call it by its initials, BOOK.

Many advantages are claimed over the old-style learning and teaching aids on which most people are brought up nowadays. It has no wires, no electric circuits to break down. No connection is needed to an electricity power plant. It is made entirely without mechanical parts to go wrong or need replacement.

Anyone can use BOOK, even children, and it fits comfortably into the hands. It can be conveniently used sitting in an armchair by the fire.

How does this revolutionary, unbelievably easy invention work? Basically BOOK consists only of a large number of paper sheets. These may run to hundreds where BOOK covers a lengthy program of information. Each sheet bears a number of sequence, so that the sheets cannot be used in the wrong order. To make it even easier for the user to keep the sheets in the proper order they are held firmly in place by a special locking device called a "binding."

Each sheet of paper presents the user with an information sequence in the form of symbols, which he absorbs optically for automatic registration on the brain. When one sheet has been assimilated a mere flick of the finger turns it over and further information is found on the other side. By using both sides of each sheet in this way, a great economy is effected, thus reducing both the size and cost of BOOK. No buttons need to be pressed to move from one sheet to another, to open or close BOOK, or to start it working.

BOOK may be taken up at any time and used by merely opening it. Instantly it is ready to use. Nothing has to be connected up or switched on. The user may turn at will to any sheet, going backward or forward as he pleases. A sheet is provided near the beginning as a location finder for any required information sequence.

A small accessory, available at trifling extra cost, is the BOOKmark. This enables the user to pick up his program where he left off on the previous learning session. BOOKmark is versatile and may be used in any BOOK.

The initial cost varies with the size and subject matter. Already a vast range of BOOKS is available, covering every conceivable subject and adjusted to different levels of aptitude. One BOOK, small enough to be held in the hands, may contain an entire learning schedule. Once purchased, BOOK requires no further cost; no batteries or wires are needed, since the motive power, thanks to the ingenious device patented by the makers, is supplied by the brain of the user.

BOOKS may be stored on handy shelves and for ease of reference the program schedule is normally indicated on the back of the binding.

Altogether the Built-in Orderly Organized Knowledge seems to have great advantages with no drawbacks. We predict a great future for it.

MAJESTIC INSTANCY

Sister Joselma, first-grade teacher in the laboratory school at Alverno College, Milwaukee, Wisconsin, wrote and published a children's book called *The Littlest Brother.*

Her pupils, who watched the book grow from stories told in class to a printed volume, were fascinated by the project. They began writing books of their own.

One was perhaps the shortest book you could find anywhere. It was composed of a sheet of paper, folded into four pages. On the front was the title *Swift Things.* Inside was a crude but lively sketch of a deer.

And beneath the deer was this penciled text: "A deer is very swift, but God is already there."

Milwaukee Journal.

CONFUSION OF TONGUES

The news editor of a large daily was doubtful about a report sent in by one of his local correspondents. It said that a farmer had lost 2,032 cows in a sudden thunderstorm. The editor picked up his phone and put in a long-distance call to the farmer. "I have a report here that says you lost two thousand thirty-two cows in the storm this morning," he said. "Is that figure correct?"

"Yeth," replied the farmer.

"Thank you," replied the editor crisply, and hung up. Then

he picked up the correspondent's report and amended it to read, "John Jones, a local farmer, lost two sows and thirty-two cows in a sudden thunderstorm this morning."

Lucille Goodyear.

A Minneapolis librarian likes to recall the boy who picked up a copy of *Trois Ours* ("The Three Bears"), the French version of the famous children's story. He carefully scanned the familiar pictures and knitted his brow thoughtfully over the unfamiliar text.

Suddenly his eyes widened. "Look at this," he exclaimed excitedly to another boy across the room. "Here's a book written in *bear* language!"

Minneapolis Star.

WHO'S IN CHARGE HERE?

An American impresario who was preparing his concert program told his new secretary routinely to expand all abbreviations—like Op. into Opus, and so on—before sending the copy to the printer.

Later, in scanning the printer's proof, he came upon this: "Bach Massachusetts in B Minor."

London Sunday Times.

CABALA

Scholars have done a good deal of research into the origins of queer languages like pidgin English; but few have paid much attention to the extraordinary language that passes between foreign correspondents and their editors. This is cablese and I am in a position to give its origin straight away: the desire to save words, and therefore money, in telegrams and cables.

There is an old-fashioned charm about this language; in some ways it goes straight back to the Middle Ages. "Canst," for example, is cheaper to say than "Can you?" A lot more money-saving discoveries have been made as time goes on, including the valuable prefix "un" which does for any kind of negative.

Let us take an imaginary example. An editor wants to tell his correspondent that, according to reports on the news agencies, serious riots have broken out near Timbuktu. He wants to know if the correspondent can book an air passage there without delay. So he cables: "Agencywise riots reportedly outbroken Timbuktuwards canst proceed airwise query." The reluctant correspondent, who is having a high old time in Cape Town or somewhere, will be all against Timbuktuwarding. He will cable back: "Viewing story upfolded Tuesday unthink coverage newsworthy." This means: "In view of the fact that the whole affair ended last Tuesday, I really think there's not much more I could say about it now." This never gets him anywhere and the next cable is always: "Proceed soonest." If he wants to fire a final shot he can only say: "Send £100 urgentest."

The classic exchange of cablese concerns a lazy correspondent who received the cable: "Why unnews query." He cabled back: "Unnews good news." His office replied: "Unnews unjob." The correspondent's final cable was too rude to be reproduced. (He lost the job anyway.)

One of my friends, isolated in some dim spot where there was no news, could get no answer to his urgent pleas for recall. He let another week go by in total silence and then suddenly cabled the one word: *Boo*. That woke them! Their instant reply was: "Boo or unboo you onstaying." But my favorite example concerns another friend whose newspaper asked him for the age of the governor of a colony that we were visiting at the time. "How old Brown," it read. He was furious. He said they could easily have got the date from the Colonial Office list in London. So he cabled back: "Old Brown fine how are you."

Lionel Fleming in the (London) Listener.

SDRAWKCAB

On many U.S. Navy ships the movie screen is suspended amidship so that it can be viewed from both sides. This procedure makes it available to larger crowds at popular movies, but usually the junior officers get a reverse image from "the wrong side of the screen."

One evening at dinnertime an enterprising young ensign passed the following word over the officers' IMC circuit: "The movie to be shown in the wardroom tonight for the senior officers is on the right side of the screen—*The Right-Handed Gun*, starring Paul Newman; and for the junior officers on the wrong side of the screen—*The Left-Handed Gun*, starring Namwen Luap."

U.S. Naval Institute Proceedings.

TAKES ALL KINDS

The Church in heaven is all saints; the Church in purgatory is all souls; the Church on earth is all sorts.

Ronald Knox.

WRONG WORDS FOR ANYBODY

Mrs. Malaprop is a character in an eighteenth-century comedy, *The Rivals*, by Richard Brinsley Sheridan. She delighted in using pretentious language to impress others. But they received the wrong impression, for she invariably misused words and made herself appear ridiculous.

The term *malapropism* has been coined in her memory. A malapropism is any glaring misuse of a word. More exactly, it is a term improperly employed through confusion with another word of similar sound or appearance.

Can you spot the malapropian blunders in the dozen sentences below?

1. In Venice people travel in gorgonzolas.
2. Anthology is the study of man.
3. Not a participle of the exploded shell could be found.
4. Flogging is not a detergent to crime.
5. The panacea is one of the vital organs of the body.
6. The mnemonic plague swept over Europe in the fourteenth century.
7. General Grunt is pleased with the enigma inscribed on his office door.
8. Her Aunt Harriet dresses ostensibly.
9. The human frame is composed of bone, sinecure, and fat.
10. Michaelangelo decorated the Pristine Chapel.
11. Today's news emulates from all over the world.
12. At the time Senator Cronk was a recumbent member of Congress.

ANSWERS TO 'WRONG WORDS FOR ANYBODY'

1. *Venetians* may occasionally travel in long, narrow canal boats called *gondolas*, but never in *gorgonzolas*. Gorgonzola is an Italian cheese.
2. *Anthropology* is the study of man. An *anthology* is a collection of poems or works of prose.
3. Perhaps no *particles* could be found after the explosion, but *participles* can be found in books of grammar. A *participle* is a word derived from a verb and having the qualities of both a verb and an adjective.
4. *Detergents* are used for cleansing. A *deterrent* may turn one away from crime.
5. The *pancreas* is a vital organ. A panacea is a supposed remedy for all ills.
6. *Bubonic* is the plague; *mnemonic* pertains to memory.
7. An *insignia*, a badge or emblem of rank, might appear on a general's door. An *enigma* is a perplexing statement, a mystery.

97

8. Some women, like Aunt Harriet, dress *ostentatiously*, rather unrefined and showy. *Ostensibly* means apparently, professedly.
9. There is *sinew*, muscular tissue, on the human frame. A *sinecure* is a profitable position requiring little work.
10. Michaelangelo is one of the artists who decorated the principal chapel in the Vatican, the *Sistine* Chapel. Something still pure or untouched, uncorrupted, can be called *pristine*.
11. News may *emanate*, come forth, issue from, all over the world, but not emulate. To try to equal or surpass is to *emulate*.
12. Unless Senator Cronk lay down or slept through sessions of Congress, he cannot be said to have been a *recumbent*. He was undoubtedly an *incumbent:* the one in office.

FLIGHTS OF FANCY

Mummies: Egyptians pressed for time—*Jane H. Clark.*

Her tongue slowed down while her thoughts rounded a curve— *Sr. M. Florian, O.S.F.*

It was a half truth, and he had the wrong half—*E. Carlson.*

Mexican weather: chili today and hot tamale—*S. J. Perelman.*

He thinks he's fit as a fiddle when he's tighter than a drum—*P. J. Norbert.*

A name that appeared to have been ladled from a bowl of alphabet soup—*Will Conway.*

Grass may grow greener on the other side of the fence, but it needs mowing more often on this side.—Successful Farming.

IV IN OUR PARISH

Illustration from *Corner Saloon*

I Built a Chapel

ह‍ॐ

BY FRANK SCULLY

I was a disintegrating thirty-eight-year-old *homo sapiens* in 1930, down to one leg, one lung, and scarcely more than one idea. If anybody had approached me on the French Riviera, where I was convalescing from a twenty-fifth operation, and told me that I would marry, become father of five children, and by 1951 be building a private chapel on the fringe of the Mojave Desert, I probably would have used what I assumed was my last breath to laugh in his face.

Recovered from the operation, and lured out to Southern California with one of those seven-year motion-picture contracts that last months, I built a home on the top of a Hollywood hill in 1936. My wife and I planned to spend the rest of our lives there. It was a dream home. We could walk an upper deck, look to the Pacific, and thus save ourselves the cost of a sea voyage. We could look north to the mountains and be glad we didn't have to climb them.

We could even look down into a parochial schoolyard a mile

away and see if our kids were playing hooky. And we could really *see* in those days. From April to November the skies were clear and the winter rains were not too devastating.

Then came the war. Heavy industry moved from the Middle West into Los Angeles. Soon the land of sunshine was a sprawling slum of smog, fog, grog, and hog-eat-hog.

Our Hollywood hill became Mount Sinus. We began retreating to the desert for short stretches to rid ourselves of cranial agonies.

Then in 1950 I had a freakish best seller which I scooped out of the flying-saucer craze. With the royalties we went hunting for a retreat beyond the smog belt. About one hundred miles east of Los Angeles on the road to Las Vegas we saw a ten-acre ranch for sale at Desert Springs. Altitude, four thousand feet. Population, 191. The ranch had eight buildings, electricity, fruit trees, shade trees, and, most important of all, water.

Up in the mountains beyond Desert Springs was a town called Wrightwood. It had a parish (twelve families) called Our Lady of the Snows. The pastor was Father Martin Dempsey, an Irish scholar who had been chief chaplain of the British forces which had reached London from Dunkirk.

He had come to California hoping to join the faculty of the University of San Diego. Although it is now the most magnificent collection of college buildings in the West, at that time not one stone had been laid upon another. So Father Dempsey was prevailed upon to take a snowbound parish two hundred miles to the north until the university became a fact.

We met Father Dempsey and became great friends with him. We asked Father to drive down with us and take a look at the ranch. He walked over the place, looked into the huge barn, chicken coops, pigpens, and corrals, asked the price, and said, "Buy it!"

Then he turned away from the desert and looked south

toward the mountains. "And we will build a chapel here," he said, pointing to a run-down ranch house, the only eyesore on the place. "We will open it next spring, May four, at nine fifteen in the morning. I'll find you some builders and will send down whatever you need for the altar."

The next spring he was there for the opening, right on time. Thereafter he would make the twenty-two mile round trip between his Wrightwood 8 A.M. and 10:30 Masses. His successor, Father Patrick Henry Linneman, also would arrive in a cloud of dust, hurrying to say our 9:15 Mass and get back to his mountain parish by 10:30.

At the time Father Dempsey ordered our chapel Desert Springs had no house of worship of any denomination. Of the 191 population three were Catholics. But the Scully Circus jumped the figure to ten and we were told there were several weekend visitors within five miles who would like a place to go to Mass.

Did you ever build a chapel? I suspect that even many priests would answer No. Some come into parishes and spend their lives ridding churchers of debts their predecessors bravely contracted. Some would not know how to whitewash a basement. Some couldn't drive a nail in a cloakroom. St. Joseph must shake his head and smile at these.

But thousands of other priests, Brothers, and nuns, especially those who have been assigned to foreign missions, know the joy of building with their own hands. I used to envy them. I envy them no more. After nine years of keeping a chapel in repair to comply with the caprices of Air-Foam Christianity, I am tired.

But in the winter and spring of 1951 the whole Scully Circus was happy working in one of God's tiniest vineyards. Everybody down to Moreen Scully (aged twenty-one months at the time) became holy hewers of wood and drawers of holy waters.

From his mountain retreat Father Dempsey sent down boxes

of linens, Mass cards, Stations of the Cross, candelabra, and other aids to a better life. Many of the objects had survived the London blitz. Some were gifts to him from Cardinal Vaughan.

He also sent down a huge embroidered drape, which was at least two hundred years old. It was to go behind the altar. It had to be lined first so that it could withstand the rigors of desert life. The gold-plated objects had to be polished. The linen and vestments had to be washed and ironed. My lady Alice, working to become the first saint of Desert Springs, did it all.

A week before our first Mass, however, the cement porch of the chapel building had not been laid and much of the painting was still undone. The exterior was painted red with white trim, but inside, the walls, which were to be a creamy yellow, and the floor, which was to be light gray, were still not done. We had converted a shower into a confessional. We installed a sliding door of the garage-door type so that everybody could see the altar from pews on the cement porch as well as from those inside.

I took all the sit-down jobs. These included staining a dozen kitchen chairs of driftwood gray and then attaching to their rear legs rubber-padded kneelers. We finished, exhausted, at eleven o'clock on Saturday night. Later that night we had to get up and find accommodations for "helpers" from Hollywood, pilgrims who had lost their way and had spent hours cruising over the Mojave Desert.

We had decided to invite everybody in the community to Mass and to breakfast. We served ninety-two breakfasts within twenty minutes after Mass.

The chapel was decorated with fresh flowers and on either side of the tabernacle was a beautifully designed bouquet of artificial flowers. Now, I can take or leave artificial flowers (and I usually leave them) but these were works of art. They were donated by Rose de Hauleville, a Belgian artist, and followed an old Flemish design. They are still there. We renew sections of them every year, but the main design remains. Rose (who is a sister-in-law of Aldous Huxley) also gave us an altar cloth which she had designed. It bore modernized images of the twelve Apostles. Finally she executed in glass a design by the Belgian Dominican Father Maas. It was a window showing the Holy Family seeking shade under a cactus plant.

Although the chapel itself had seating accommodations for fourteen, we had more than sixty for our opening Mass, some on the porch and others standing in the sun. All, however, could see the altar.

The non-Catholic husband of a visiting lady gave us invaluable help. A carpenter, he offered to build the altar railing. He asked Father Dempsey where he should put it. Father, not a very tall man, went to the altar, genuflected, and said, "Just back of my foot!"

It is a pretty piece of work, stained, like the chairs, a driftwood gray. But we always have to tell tall priests who come to say Mass to genuflect sideways, or they will get banged.

Before the opening Mass we were trying to figure out how to have everything ready, including breakfast. Father Dempsey knew a couple he was sure would help. He brought them down from Wrightwood the day before. They were Mr. and Mrs. Clarence Drury. They came with a skillet and spatula each and took over the kitchen so efficiently that our worries were ended for all subsequent opening Masses and breakfasts.

Our Lady of the Desert is in the San Diego diocese, which must be about the largest in the United States. It's as large as all Ireland. Bishop Charles F. Buddy of San Diego graciously gave permission for the Blessed Sacrament to remain with us as long as we were on the ranch.

That opening Mass, though early in May, was greeted with a most heavenly day. It was warm; not a leaf stirred; multicolored desert flowers lay like a fifty-mile carpet from the steps of our Lady's chapel to the foothills. Two hundred miles beyond, Mount Whitney stood clear in the snow.

It was the third Sunday after Easter. The Epistle was St. Peter's: "I exhort you as strangers and as pilgrims." We were all pilgrims and strangers at Desert Springs that sunny spring morning.

Magnificent churches have often had such humble beginnings, Father Dempsey explained. No church, when you got down to the essentials, has more than the Blessed Sacrament, a sanctuary light, the Stations of the Cross, the crucifix, an altar, and a tabernacle; Our Lady of the Desert had all these.

Of course, we had a few problems. We learned that a sign on the main road would result in a $2 tax, so we moved it far enough back to get out of the way of the state's tax collectors. (This may have been a small contribution to the separation of Church and State, but at least it was a contribution.)

Once, after we had been working on a boy for some weeks, we finally got him to want to go to Confession, only to discover that the priest who was saying Mass that morning was from a neighboring diocese and that his faculties did not extend to ours.

The county line was a mile away. "Listen, Father," I said, "would you mind driving him over to your side of the county line? It's important that this boy go to Confession today." The priest thought it was a good idea.

On another occasion a Sister of Social Service came thundering down the mountainside driving a truck. She was delivering a priest as a substitute for Father Dempsey, whose health had gradually been breaking down.

After she had introduced the priest she turned back and said, "Oh, I forgot to tell you—Father can't speak a word of English!" He was a visitor from Germany and had been in the country only ten days. The universality of the Church was clearly illustrated in this instance. Until he said the prayers after Mass, nobody in the chapel suspected that he wasn't an American.

Father Dempsey died in 1953, but we always think of Our Lady of the Desert as his chapel. In fact, it was he who told us it was not a "private chapel" but a "public oratory." Only the family could be considered as having attended Mass in a private chapel, whereas a public oratory would fulfill the obligation for anyone, even a passing stranger, who attended Mass. After that we put out signs: "Visitors Welcome."

Since 1951 hundreds of tired travelers have been refreshed at Our Lady of the Desert. Last summer twenty-three Masses were celebrated by visiting priests within three weeks. On two occasions we had four Masses in one day. Sometimes whole families have come off the highway to visit, say a family Rosary, and then drive on.

Have we found any thorns on this desert rose? Yes, a few. One woman suggested that the reason more people did not attend Mass was that the kneelers were terrible. Since I had made them and had never once heard our Lord whisper, "My, my, can't you do better than that?" I was inclined to file the critic among the carpers. The kneelers were padded with rubber for knees which had long since given up scrubbing floors, but it is possible they were too close to the rear of the chair to which they were attached. The worshipers were forced to kneel straight up instead of slouching on their haunches, and perhaps the erect posture was tiring.

We visited churches in town, measuring pews and kneelers, and found that some were better and some were worse than ours. Then one day we fell heir to some old pews and kneelers. The kneelers had to be restuffed and re-covered, and some of the pews had to be sawed in half because they were too long for our little public oratory.

Does having the Blessed Sacrament where you live bring a greater sense of intimacy or familiarity? Well, that can be best judged by how the children react. One night after we had said our prayers in the chapel, Moreen, then about two, waved back at the altar and said, "Good night, Goddie."

Another time she said, "Good night, God, take good care of Yourself."

Her mother replied, "He's all right, but we aren't."

"If He's all right," she demanded with pint-sized indignation, "then why is He wearing a cross?"

Thus far, only one miracle has been reported as remotely connected with Our Lady of the Desert. The miracle is that I had anything to do with it.

We all hope, though, that our little chapel will produce some St. Pauls in time and thereby gain the revered status of a shrine. After all, our desert road looks a lot like the road to Damascus.

GOOD JOHNNY

A four-year-old boy was inevitably an imp at church every Sunday, but the congregation was very much surprised last Sunday. The Introit passed, the Collects, the Epistle, and there hadn't been a sound from the boy—in fact, he had barely moved.

Just as the Gospel was ending the parishioners near him heard him whisper softly, "Daddy." About a minute later he repeated it a little louder, and then a third time, but his father persisted in ignoring him.

By the time the sermon was under way almost everyone at Mass could hear the boy calling, "Daddy!" audibly but not disturbingly.

Finally, however, the boy's patience was exhausted. "Daddy!" he shouted at the top of his voice. "Daddy, I'm being good!"

Lawrence W. Murphy.

RECESS

Our pastor delights in talking to little children. They love him for it, for he never talks down to them.

One day he spent an especially long time with the first graders at recess. The next morning his housekeeper answered the doorbell. Two little tots asked her hopefully, "Can monsignor come out and play?"

M.F.

MERRY CHRISTMAS

The first graders were learning "Jingle Bells." At the line "Bells on bobtails ring," Sister thought she heard something strange from one little girl. She had her repeat the song and, sure enough, the girl had brought the song up to date. It was now, "Bells and cocktails ring."

Dorothy M. Fleming.

CORNER SALOON

A nun traveling on a bus forgot the name of the street where she was to get out. She was panic-stricken for a moment, but then she suddenly remembered a well-known landmark one block away.

Before a busload of startled passengers Sister called out to the driver, "Please let me off at Tracey's Tavern.

Sister Ruth Thérèse.

109

OOPS

A missioner told his congregation that the following week he would preach on lying. He asked them in the meantime to read the seventeenth chapter of the Gospel of St. Mark.

The next Sunday he asked from the pulpit how many had done the reading he had assigned. A number of hands went up. "I see," said the missioner. "You are the very people I wish to reach. There is no seventeenth chapter in Saint Mark's Gospel."

The Sower.

DEALER

When Johnny, our first-grader, brought home his October report card, we weren't very happy to see it. Among other disappointing grades we saw that he had a *D* in deportment. I was all ready to administer a tongue-lashing, but his father persuaded me to accentuate the positive. So the next morning as I signed the card I said, "Look, Johnny, if you are able to bring up that grade in deportment, I'll give you a whole dollar!"

Johnny was delighted. He went off happily to school that morning and when the other kids went out for recess, he stayed behind to talk to Sister. "Look, Sister," he began brightly, "would you like to make fifty cents?"

Mrs. B. Reiley.

KEEP ON THE GRASS

At St. Peter's in Memphis, Tennessee, a sign painter made up a little sign and presented it to the church.

The sign was promptly placed in the little garden where priests and visitors stroll. It read, "Trespassers will be forgiven."

Vincent Barba.

CONSTITUTIONAL PROCEDURE

At the height of the segregation storm the parents of a first-grader sent her off for her first day at a newly integrated school. When the school closed in the afternoon, the mother met the youngster at the door with the car. "How did everything go, honey?" she inquired.

"Oh, mother! You know what? A little Negro girl sat next to me!" the youngster exclaimed.

Afraid that this might mark a traumatic experience that would need explaining, the mother asked, "And what happened?"

"We were both so scared that we held hands all day," the child explained.

Mrs. Joseph Felice.

FORWARD

Little Mary was telling us the story of Lot's wife one Sunday morning as we were driving to church. "Our Sister says that God told Lot's wife not to look back, but she did, and He immediately turned her into a statue of salt," she related. Then very seriously she said, "I wouldn't look back."

"That's a good girl," said her father, proud of her sense of obedience. "What would you do?"

"I'd look up there," Mary answered, pointing up to the rear-view mirror.

E.B.

ITE MISSA EST

After Mass one Sunday my little girl dropped my hand and vanished among the congregation.

I heard her calling me frantically, "Hannah! Hannah! Hannah!"

When I found her, I scolded her. "You shouldn't let go my hand," I said, "and you shouldn't call me 'Hannah.' I'm 'mother' to you, dear."

"I know, mother," she wailed, "but the whole church is full of mothers!"

Hannah Mullen.

BUSY BODIES

Sister was teaching her first grade the story of the Pharisees and the spirit of hypocrisy. Then she was suddenly called from the classroom for a few minutes.

When she returned she found the children all busily engaged at their desks. "My, what good children!" she remarked.

One girl timidly raised her hand. "Yes, Claire," said Sister, "what is it?"

Claire shyly replied, "Oh, Sister, we are hypocrites."

Sister Mary Agnita, C.PP.S.

CAPTIVE AUDIENCE

I had been saving diocesan newspapers for one of the paper drives held often in our neighborhood.

When a little girl came to the door collecting, I told her, "I have a bunch of *Long Island Catholics* tied up in the attic, and another bunch in the cellar."

She gave me a frightened look, edged away, and said, "They're awfully quiet, aren't they?" Then she ran.

Mrs. Vincent H. Dwyer.

SEPTET

Our pastor was trying hard to organize a choir. After a few weeks of dubious response he made this announcement at Sunday Mass: "Everybody in the parish is willing to have a choir. Seven are willing to sing in it. The rest are willing to let them."

Leonard J. Schreifels.

TRANSLATION

In Namanyere, Tanzania, the children understand the Latin responses of the Mass very well. When the priest first used the vernacular language for "The Lord be with you," seven-year-old Petro whispered to his younger brother, "That means *Dominus vobiscum.*"

E. Guerts, W.F.

ALL TOGETHER NOW

My grandmother was at first reluctant to join in singing hymns at Mass. For several Sundays she stood closemouthed while the rest of us sang along with amateur gusto. Then one Sunday I detected her quavering voice amid the chorus.

Later in the day I asked her about her change of heart. "It's not that I'm much for the singing," she said. "But it's a darn sight better than listening."

Roberta Brault.

PARTICIPATION

Congregational participation in the liturgy is making an impression, at least on the younger generation. When one five-year-old was asked, "Who said Mass this morning?" she replied, "We all did."

Ida Kosciesza.

ECUMENICAL COLLECTION

One Sunday a friend, curious about the Mass, asked if he could accompany me that day to church. We sat in one of the back pews. After a few minutes the head usher tapped me on the shoulder and asked if my friend and I would help with the Sunday collection. I pointed out that my friend was a stranger in town, but he wouldn't take No for an answer. At the back of the church he gave us some quick instructions. At first I was worried, but soon I beamed proudly as I watched my friend march down his aisle, genuflect in unison with the other ushers, and pass the basket. He did this not for one collection, but for the second collection as well, and both times he did just fine!

Neither the pastor nor the head usher will ever know that the two gentlemen who helped with the collection that day were one Catholic and one Jew!

Anthony Cannata.

FLIGHTS OF FANCY

One of those Catholics who goes to late o'clock Mass—*Richard Keolker.*
Altar boy with a six-foot wing span—*Kathleen L. Niles.*
Communion breakfast: homily and grits—*Donald F. Barkman.*
A spoke trying to look like a wheel—*Maurice Seitter.*

V SMALL FRY

Illustration from *Kids Have the Answers*

Kids Have the Answers

ह∾

BY HAROLD DUNN

Did you know that digestion is best accomplished on an empty stomach? That vitamins are easier to say than what they mean? Or that chicken pox has a plural known as poultry?

I have gleaned this information from examinations and essays during nine years of teaching. Some of the kids' comments about health are hilarious; all are in the delightful style of children.

One intense fourth grader's interest in health resulted in, "Vitamins are to take when they are not to talk about on television."

"I already know the proper way to brush teeth is not sideways. I always brush my teeth upside and down."

I'm convinced that our funniest entertainers are in grade school. Only an unconscious little comedian could say, "Mr. Penicillin taught us that the best way to keep healthy is to eat moldy bread."

There is usually an element of truth in the wackiest answer. Sometimes the youngsters aren't wrong at all; it's just the way

117

they put it: "Medicine has made wonderful strides lately. Although people still die, they don't die so quick." "A good thing to remember about swimming after eating is don't." "Green persimmons are a rich source of indigestion."

Whenever grade schoolers discuss medicines, boners usually pop up all over the page. "The benefit of iodine is if a person hurts himself he can drink some to stop the pain." "An anecdote is medicine we all have to take."

Anecdote—antidote; when a mere couple of misplaced letters completely change the meaning of a word, what chance do kids have?

Other misunderstood words led to: "Meningitis is caused by your spinal cord and brain being too informed"; "In Washington's time they believed in bleeding sick people. Today we know we should give them blood plaster."

Ever heard of the word *oinkment?* I hadn't until I came across this gem: "Oinkment is to put on rags to put off colds."

I've been trying to figure this one out for five years. Question: Have you been vaccinated for smallpox? Answer: No. I am single.

Another one of the questionnaires had this information. Question: Have you been vaccinated for influenza this year? If so, where? Answer: Yes. The usual place.

Sometimes the kids don't know and they know they don't know, but that doesn't keep their answers from being charming: "An artery carries the blood to or from the heart. I forget which, but the body remembers, and that is the important thing."

Once I explained that germs are too small to be seen without the aid of a microscope. So how did it come out in a test paper the next day? "Germs are smaller than a necked eye."

The same chap also supplied me with this bit of information:

"The meaning of strepticockeye is only for the doctor to have whispered in his ear."

The brain comes in for its share of comment from youngsters: "Every time we think, the brain gets all electroded. But this don't hurt because we don't feel nothing up there."

The appendix has elicited such information as this. "An appendix is something found in the back of a book. Sometimes they get in people and have to be taken out."

Youngsters certainly have their own opinions and few hesitate to express them. "After seeing an optomist, many people have found that their eyes and headaches have disappeared. And you don't have to take your clothes off." Or, "A quack doctor is one who specializes in treating lame ducks."

One of my students this year has had many tussles with his spelling book. When he finished writing a sentence recently, the battleground looked like this: "The number of axidents in America each day is an adsurbly hugh fact of a number."

Tonsils naturally catch their attention: "Tonsilitis is a spare word for when you can't think how to say sore throat." Or, "A tonsorial is a place where they take out your tonsils."

Some fifth graders deal with more serious ailments: "Hoof-in-mouth disease is something orators get. We usually have to shoot them." "Streptomycin is one of our most essential diseases." "We will have eliminated all the childish diseases in a few hundred years. Just wait and see."

Much of my information is related to effective first aid: "If anybody cut his leg real bad, I would take it to the nearest doctor." "Whenever somebody swallows something down the wrong way, you ought to slap him on the back until he is dead."

In an essay "Accidents and First Aids," a tiny moppet seemed able to think of only one good first-aid rule, but she played it for all it was worth: "The four things you should do for someone if you do not know where he is hurt are: 1. Be sure not to move him. 2. If he asks to go to a hospital, tell him in a minute but don't move him. 3. Let him talk unless he wants to move around. 4. If you or he are cold you can get some hot chochlet, but fix it so he can't move."

Here's some sage advice about accident prevention. "Many autobomile accidents are caused by lack of stopping. Like if a brake stops working, don't try to go on. When anybody gets to a stopping place, he should stop."

OK, I can take a hint.

IN OUR HOUSE

After I had been hounding him about it for three months, my eight-year-old son at long last got around to thanking his aunt for a Christmas gift. "Dear Auntie," he wrote, "I'm sorry I didn't thank you before for my Christmas present and it would serve me right if you forgot all about my birthday, which is next Saturday."

Ernest Blevins.

WHEREVER

On her first day of school little Debbie began to cry.

"You aren't homesick already, are you?" Sister asked kindly.

"No," was the tearful response. "I'm *here* sick."

V. D. P.

LIGHTED UP

Youngsters do brighten up a home. Which one of them ever turns off the lights?

Christian Herald.

ROUND AND ROUND

Little Laura was lying on the floor on her back singing a happy song. When mother next glanced at her, Laura was lying on her stomach, shrilling another song.

"Playing a game, dear?" mother asked.

"Yes," replied the child. "I'm pretending I'm a phonograph record, and I've just turned myself over."

V. D. Palat.

BIG BULB

During a summer storm a flash of lightning and a violent thunderclap scared the wits out of me. Although I did not want our five-year-old Philip to develop a fear of storms, I involuntarily exclaimed, "Oh, that lightning!"

But Philip had been charmed rather than scared. "I thought," he explained, "that God was taking our picture."

Mrs. Charles Branon.

THE ANSWER MAN

A parochial-school science class was being given a final examination. One of the questions was, "Which are the last teeth to appear in the mouth?"

One youngster's succinct answer: "False."

Coronet.

COUNTDOWN

I was working in our garage when my five-year-old son Mike, tired from playing with his little friends, came in and sat down near the door. In a few minutes eight-year-old Billy, a neighbor boy, came stealing in; he kept glancing nervously over his shoulder. "Get your guns, Mike," he whispered.

"Why?" asked Mike.

"Tommy says he's giving us just until he counts to one hundred to get out of town."

"Oh, that's OK," replied Mike. "We don't have to leave. Tommy can't count to one hundred."

Robert Yoho in Coronet.

KID STUFF

When my infant daughter developed a rash on her neck, my five-year-old daughter overheard me saying that I was going to take her to a baby doctor. She tugged at my skirt to get my attention, then asked in a curious tone, "How *big* is the baby doctor?"

Yvonne Wilcox.

CHARIVARIA

On his first day of kindergarten Paul drew a picture of a stagecoach.

"That's very well done, Paul," the teacher remarked encouragingly, "but I don't see any wheels. What holds it up?"

"Bad men," replied Paul.

S. J. Gudge.

BUT PLENTY OF CAVITIES

My neighbors had given their son Willie a bicycle and were watching proudly as he rode around and around the block.

On his first circuit Willie shouted: "Look, Mom, no hands!"

The second time around: "Look, Mom, no feet!"
The third time: "Look, Mom, no teeth!"

S. J. Gudge.

DEUS IN MACHINA

Little Sue was taking her first train ride. When night came her parents saw her into an upper berth and then retired to their own quarters in another section. Alone and a little frightened, Sue called out at intervals: "Daddy, are you there? Mamma, are you there?"

After this had gone on for some time, an irritable old gentleman called out in a gruff voice: "Yes, Daddy is here. Mamma is here. I am here. We are all trying to sleep. Now, settle down, and for heaven's sake, stop making that noise!"

There was a long silence. Then a thin little voice called out, "Daddy, was that God?"

Quote.

PREFACE

Michael took a long time to show his report card to his mother and dad. "Perhaps I'd better explain it first," he said. "*A* stands for excellent. *B* means good. *C* is fair. And *D* is what I got."

J. J. Kelly.

KID STUFF

Three-year-old Melissa and her mother sometimes visited our convent. One day, when it was time for mother to leave, little Melissa could not be found. She was finally discovered on the back-porch steps, stroking the convent cat.

"Come along, Melissa, it's time we were going," Mother told her.

"Yes, Mother," she replied dutifully. "But I don't know what to do about this cat. He has his motor running."

Sister Cesira, F.M.A.

POSITIVELY NEGATIVE

A little boy kept asking his mother, "But why can't I have a popsicle?"

His mother replied severely, "Because you asked for it in a negative way—that's why."

Morris Bender.

REWARDS OF EFFORT

Teaching third-grade catechism often affords me an opportunity to test my sense of humor. One morning I was listening to prayers and awarding gold stars for each one said correctly when the box slipped out of my hand. Gold stars descended like confetti all over the floor. I got down on my hands and knees and attempted to insert my fingernails under the tiny gold stickers, conscious all the while of what an undignified picture I must be presenting.

Finally I looked up and said sharply, "Isn't anyone going to give me a hand?" Immediately all twenty-four of my pupils began to applaud enthusiastically.

Mrs. Bernard J. Sexton.

SAY WHAT YOU MEAN

While I was preparing the laundry my small daughter threw her red socks into a basket of clothes. When I asked her not to because they might run, she gave me a disgusted look and demanded, "How can they run when they have no feet in them?"

Mary Parr.

BEGINNER

After returning an overdue book at the public library, a small boy stood at the desk with his past-due notice in one hand and his fine in the other. After he paid his fine he asked, "Please, can I have the letter back? It's the first one I ever got."

Coronet.

HOW COME

On his first trip to the zoo a little boy stared at a stork for a while, then turned to his father and remarked, "Gee, Dad, he doesn't recognize me!"

Grand Rapids Press.

ATTRACTION AND COMPULSION

Willie had been playing truant from school and had spent a long, beautiful day fishing. On his way back he met one of his young cronies who asked him, "Catch anything?"

"Ain't been home yet," replied Willie.

C. Kennedy.

COMPLIMENTARY

As I entered a child's hospital room, I heard a relative say, "Susie, you're a pretty sick girl."

"Thank you," said Susie, "but I'm prettier when I'm well."

Mrs. D. Binder.

BUG SHOE

My little Cathy was discussing different types of "grown-up" shoes with her playmate who asked what pointed-toed shoes were good for.

"They're just right for stepping on bugs in corners," Cathy replied.

Christine Davis.

EMILY POSTMANSHIP

Little Bobby had just returned from a birthday party. His mother asked, "Bobby, did you thank the lady for the party?"

"Well, I was going to," the little boy replied. "But a girl ahead of me said, 'Thank you,' and the lady told her not to mention it. So I didn't."

Mrs. J. Felice.

THE MAN WHO

A little boy came down to the docks with his parents to greet his big brother who was returning from overseas duty. In the confusion the parents couldn't see their favorite soldier, but somehow the youngster managed to pick him out. "There he is!" the boy shouted, pointing up at the big transport.

"Where?" demanded the father.

The youngster pointed to a porthole high in the side of the ship. "Up there," he said, "with the boat around his neck!"

Rays of Sunshine.

SOUND OF MUSIC

My neighbor's four-year-old sat next to me on the piano bench as I played a lullaby.

"Pretty sounds, pretty sounds," she quietly observed.

"Do you think music is the prettiest sound?" I asked.

"No," she said thoughtfully. "Laughing is the prettiest sound."

Mrs. S. Lee.

CHANTICLEER

Little Dwight is a city boy but he likes to visit his grandparents who live on a farm. One day when he was coming out of the barn where he had gathered a few eggs, a rooster came up behind him and crowed.

"Thank you," Dwight replied politely, "but I'm already up."

Marcia Bougine.

DELAYED ACTION

A small boy had just had a heartbreaking experience while playing and had gone into the house with tears in his eyes.

Just then his father tooted the car horn and asked him if he would like to go for a ride. The small boy turned to his mother and said, "Just wipe my tears away. I'll finish crying when I get back!"

C. Kennedy.

STICKY CHRISTMAS

Last Christmas little Janine Stewart, age four, was going around the house singing at full voice her favorite Christmas carol: "Slick the walls with bowls of jelly! Fa-la-la-la-la-la-la-la-la!"

St. Paul Pioneer Press.

FLIGHTS OF FANCY

Little Mary, suffering her first attack of hiccups: "Mama, mama, I'm percolating!"—*Charles Chick Govin.*

Little boy, on being presented with a stuffed dog: "But I wanted one that was made out of dog."—*Ernest Blevins.*

Children rushing home at half past hungry—*Mary C. Dorsey.*

Clinging-whine type—*Mary C. Dorsey.*

Exercising shelf control in supermarkets—*Irene Warsaw.*

Children boomeranging home from kindergarten—*Terry.*

Two dimples tacked her smile in place—*Paul Bell.*

VI THE GOOD SHEPHERD AND THE ANIMAL FLOCK

Illustration from *Animals Have Their Fun*

Pope John XXIII

ॐ

BY BARRETT McGURN

An orange moon rose over the Tiber in the black of an early fall evening in Rome. We waited in front of St. Peter's Basilica for our first glimpse of the new Pope. Eighty-five-year-old Cardinal Canali had just announced that we "had a Pope," and that he was the former Angelo Giuseppe Cardinal Roncalli, Patriarch of Venice, now John XXIII.

Five cardinals in bright orange-red crowded shoulder to shoulder in the window to the left of the balcony high on St. Peter's façade. Ten more pressed forward on the right. Finally thirty-five appeared together. Until an hour before, the cardinals, acting as a unit, had been the supreme organ of the Church. Now the immense responsibility was another's. One who had been their equal and brother was the new Holy Father of all.

A white figure appeared at the center of the balcony. "I know, I know," we could hear him saying in Italian to those who were fussing and whispering at his elbow. The microphone was alive. "I know." The voice was gentle but assured.

For me it was the first sight of the former Cardinal Roncalli, though I had covered the Vatican as an American newsman for nearly a decade. It was professionally upsetting to realize that one so important had escaped my attention, but I was comforted to learn that even many of the cardinals had known little about him. Yet when days of discussion and prayers for inspiration were over so many of the cardinals had converged their votes on the Patriarch of Venice that he had accepted election as the manifest will of God.

Who was this man on whom the cardinals had agreed?

Days of quick interviewing brought this picture. The man who had risen to such honor and responsibility was one who had never sought them. "From the time I was born," he told a friend, "I had never had any thought but to be a country priest." He was the son of a poor farmer in the Alpine foothills of northern Italy.

Angelo Roncalli had been chosen after ordination to be secretary of his bishop, Count Giacomo Radini-Tedeschi. Later he had been called to Rome to direct the Italian national Society for the Propagation of the Faith under Pius XI. At forty-four he had been sent abroad and had served for nearly thirty years as a papal diplomat. In 1953 he had been called back to Italy as Cardinal Patriarch of Venice.

He had been nuncio, or ambassador, of the papal court to France for nine years when he heard that his promotion to the College of Cardinals was imminent. The appointment meant leaving a post where his gentle thoughtfulness had worked diplomatic wonders, winning him the goodwill of Catholics and bitter anticlericals alike. The cardinal-to-be had written to his niece, a missionary nun in Africa, telling her that he hoped for no such advancement. "My little boat seems to float well here on the waters of the Seine," he said.

Before he became Patriarch of Venice, it was predicted that the nuncio would be summoned to direct one of the Vatican congregations. As he skimmed through *Figaro*, the Paris morning paper, one day, the nuncio was struck by a picture of the "gondola of death," the boat-hearse which had just carried Venice's Archbishop Carlo Agostini to his island grave. The nuncio folded the clipping into his breviary as a memento. Within days he received his notification that he was the new Patriarch of Venice.

After twenty-eight years as a diplomat he was to be shepherd of 300,000 souls. "I know of no finer assignment for a man than to be a pastor," he told his people on his arrival in Venice.

To Angelo Roncalli's lifelong desire to be a good shepherd was joined an infectious goodwill and warmth which the cardinals must have observed in their days before the final vote. We of the world press saw it as John XXIII gave us an audience two days after his coronation.

He told us conversationally that in these days of sudden new burdens he should have been getting sleep at night, but that he had been plagued by insomnia. And those long hours of the night had been dedicated to us. He had been reading through piles of newspapers to see how we had been covering the Church's crucial event. Reporter after reporter had been trying to pry into the secrets of the election, secrets which none but the Pope can divulge without incurring grave penalties.

"Not two lines" of the guesses were right, the Pope chided, with evident amusement. One could respect the reporters for their determined enterprise in trying to get the big news, he said, but one had to admire the cardinals even more for the skill with which they had guarded the secrets. It was gratifying to us journalists to see that the Holy Father understood our problems.

Pope John's origins were as humble as those of Abraham Lincoln. "We were very poor, but we never knew we lacked anything," the diplomat once recalled. "But then," he added, "we really *didn't* lack anything."

Sausage and cornmeal were the bulk of the family diet. There were never cakes or even the omnipresent Italian wine. Sotto il

Monte, where Angelo Roncalli was born, had no schooling beyond the third grade. But the pious farmer's family got by. When the new Pope was lifted aloft for the first time on the papal *sedia gestatoria*, the portable throne, he thought of how his father, Giovanni, had carried him on his shoulders a long distance when he was seven to attend a Catholic Action rally.

Those early days have never left the Pope's mind. As Patriarch of Venice he continued to vacation in Sotto il Monte. When his aides would protest that he was emptying his pockets of their last *lire* to meet the demands of beggars his answer was, "No matter how little is left, it will be more than my father had."

When the president of France, Vincent Auriol, asked whom the cardinal designate would like present at the ceremony for the conferring of his red hat as a prince of the Church, his immediate reply was, "The mayor of Sotto il Monte."

Most of the postwar premiers of France were present on that occasion. One of the nuncio's most striking traits (and a most profoundly influential trait where non-Catholics were concerned) was his ability to get along on gracious terms with men of all beliefs or none. Everyone was welcome to his cordial conversation—even the Soviet ambassador, Mr. Boromolov, with whom he was photographed in a placid exchange.

President Auriol was an anticlerical socialist. Yet when Pius XII designated the nuncio as a cardinal, Auriol said that he as president would present the red hat in accordance with the ancient custom in Catholic countries.

"He kneels not to me, an unbeliever, but through me to the Pope," Auriol explained in confusion. Then, touched deeply, the president murmured to the new cardinal, "It is we who should kneel to you, Your Eminence."

"I have sought always what united, not what divided," Cardinal Roncalli once remarked. That policy of his has been given credit for a surprising event in France. When the nuncio's old friend Edouard Herriot, a famous anticlerical statesman, lay dying, he asked for a Church blessing.

Pope John is a man of lively wit. Once, while he was nuncio in Paris, he was discussing the fables of the French writer La Fontaine. He remarked that everybody in the world, premiers, diplomats, factory owners, clerks, even poor hoboes on the banks of the Seine, could find their counterparts in La Fontaine.

A sly reporter asked him which animal character in the fables corresponded to the nuncio.

"Myself?" he said, smiling. "You will forgive a diplomat if he refuses to give away the key to the strongbox in which he keeps his secrets."

He is a man of courage. In Venice they tell of the day when communists demonstrated before the patriarchate. Police telephone to ask whether the cardinal wanted protection. He refused. A little later the patriarch stepped out into the crowd with his familiar affable smile. The Red crowd simmered down. Moments later it dispersed.

Elevation to the papal throne did not find John unprepared. As Patriarch of Venice, and one of those who would vote for Pius XII's successor, he wrote to his seminarians about what they should seek in their prayers: "A wise and gentle ruler: a saint, and one who will bring others to sanctity."

To us newspapermen in that audience just after the coronation John elaborated on this point. The Pope should not be thought of as a diplomat, or a "political Pope," or a "scholar Pope." All those qualities were desirable "embellishments," but nothing more. The Pope's true task was to be "a good shepherd."

Every day that has followed the election of Pope John XXIII has made clearer the reasons why the cardinals chose Angelo Roncalli to succeed Pius XII as "good shepherd."

Animals Have Their Fun

୧ଈ

BY DAL STIVENS

Explorer Carl Akeley was attracted by strange trumpeting from a herd of elephants ahead of him in the jungle. He crept near and was spellbound by what he saw. The elephants were milling round a three-foot ball of sunbaked earth. With their trunks and feet they were shoving it this way and that along the ground in an elephantine version of soccer. The cries the beasts were uttering, Akeley realized, were not of alarm or anger but of excited pleasure. They seemed like small boys playing football.

Bears like games, too. Several persons have seen grizzlies climb to the top of snow-clad slopes and toboggan down on their haunches. At the bottom the bears shook the snow from their fur and began the dogged climb again—no bear has yet devised a snow lift.

It is foolish to attribute our own emotions to animals. Animals are *not* like us. Yet in these instances it is clear the animals *were* having fun and were *playing*.

136

Some animal play is a form of learning. I once watched young weasels making quick dives and feints at each other. They were instinctively practicing how to catch small rodents and fish. When they became too fierce, the mother weasel would interfere with warning snarls.

Adult males supervise the play of young howling monkeys and stop the scuffles with a grunt if they become too rough. Howling monkeys like to wrestle upside down, hanging by their tails.

Boxing is a pastime of young raccoons, badgers, and kangaroos. This again, particularly for kangaroos, is preparation for the strenuous male combats of later life.

The games of some adult animals are closely identified with their way of life. Foxes and coyotes will toss a stick into the air and catch it. They will worry it, set it down, walk away, and then stalk and make a swift lunge at it. Such play could be surplus energy finding a near-at-hand outlet. But it is like their normal hunting life. (Dogs that delight in fetching sticks are substituting a game for their old, wild ancestral life.)

Even a solemn-looking animal like the hippopotamus likes to play. One in the Amsterdam zoo made a toy out of a maple leaf which drifted into his tank one day. He swam under the leaf and blew a fine puff of air that carried the leaf upward out of the water. When the leaf alighted, the hippopotamus puffed it up again. He kept up the game for hour after hour.

Some animal games parallel our own. Red deer play tag. When the deer that is "it" catches another, he reaches out and tags him with his hoof! Some deer play what looks like hide-and-seek, stalking one another around a hill.

Animals having their fun can give humans some anxious moments. On a bright moonlit night on the Argentine pampas, the naturalist W. H. Hudson was sleeping on the ground when he was suddenly awakened by the cry of a puma. In the white glare he now saw four of the great cats coming toward him. Tense and terrified, Hudson held his breath. Then, while he lay motionless, they took turns jumping over his body! After five minutes of this high-blooded fun they wandered off into the night.

Dolphins indulge in mischief. At Florida State University's marine laboratories they zip up from the depth to smack snoozing sea birds with their tail flukes. They also like to nibble at the fins of sleeping fish and have been known to overturn turtles with their snouts. Another favorite game is to pluck a floating feather and then try to balance it on their noses.

Birds clearly delight in games. Once in Australia I watched two eagles play with a large stick. First the male would soar high in the air and let the stick go; when it had dropped a hundred feet or so, the female would come swooping down and catch it in midair. In turn she would soar aloft and drop the stick for the male.

Naturalist David Fleay had a trained hunting wedge-tailed eagle called Horatio that put on a turn whenever a favorite visitor came. She would fling bones upward with a twist of her beak and grab them as they fell. Her attempt to impress visitors also extended to a little nest building, just to show how versatile she could be.

Another predator, the little falcon of Australia, likes to amuse itself by buzzing slow-flying, large birds such as the ibis. Obviously the little falcon has no chance of striking down so large a bird. It makes its plunging dives out of the sun for the sport of seeing the great birds tumbling, weaving, and taking evasive action. It is not difficult to imagine the falcon chuckling maliciously at the panic it causes.

Dancing plays an important part in the courtship of many birds; among some it appears to have developed further into communal fun. Razorbills do a paddle dance on the surface of the sea. They swim in single file and then converge in a circle until their beaks almost touch. The circle swells and then breaks. The birds bow and come together to hold beaks and waltz around each other in pairs. Then they form a single line with beaks and tails raised. As one observer puts it, "It is as good a description of a folk dance as any I have ever heard. It seems to be pure enjoyment of rhythmic patterns of motion."

Animals do, indeed, have their fun, in the words of W. H. Hudson, "periodical fits of gladness."

QUESTION OF LOYALTY

Young Steve's first four months at kindergarten apparently had widened his horizons considerably, so his mother thought it would be interesting to inquire about his current loyalties.

"Honey," she said, "whom do you love the best?"

Soberly he considered the question and then replied, "Well, I love you best. And then comes Daddy. And teacher is last. But in between come a lot of dogs."

F. Frangart.

THE DISAPPROVERS

The prodigal son was the subject of the catechism lesson and Sister was dwelling on the character of the elder brother.

"But amid all the enjoyment," said Sister, "there was one to whom the preparation of the feast brought no joy; to whom the prodigal's return gave no happiness, only bitterness; one who did not approve of the feast and who had no wish to attend it.

"Now who can tell me who this was?"

Silence for several moments, then a hand was raised and a small, sympathetic voice said, "Please, Sister, it was the fatted calf."

The Scapular.

PLAYMATES

A four-year-old Milwaukee youngster walked into his home one day carrying a worm. "What," demanded his horrified mother, "are you doing with that worm?"

"We were playing outside," the boy said, "and I thought I'd show him my room."

Doyle K. Getter in the Milwaukee Journal.

THE HUNGRY CRITICS

Two nanny goats were grazing in a Hollywood dump; one nuzzled out a reel of film and the two chewed meditatively on the tasty morsel for several seconds. Then the first goat said to the second goat, "Isn't this just too yummy for words?"

"Well, it's a nice bit," conceded the second goat. "But on the whole I think I liked the book better."

Minneapolis Tribune.

THE VET

We have acquired a new kitten at our house and the children were quite concerned when I told them he was due for his distemper shots. I explained that they were good for the kitty and were kind of like the polio shots that they had been given. They thought, then, that we should take the kitten to our family doctor.

Again I explained that he was a doctor just for people and that we would have to take Chipper to an animal doctor.

This satisfied the older children, but our five-year-old Rita was still suspicious.

"What kind of an animal is he?" she wanted to know.

Mrs. James W. Hawkins.

THE SECRET

A lady who prided herself on her housekeeping was horrified when she saw a mouse run across her living-room floor. Calling her daughter, she said, "Hurry down to the hardware store and buy some mousetraps."

Then she added, "But for goodness' sake, don't tell them what we want them for!"

The Far East.

FRIGHTFUL

The Sister who teaches the third grade took her pupils to visit the zoo. Their assignment was to take notes on the animals they saw and prepare written reports for the principal. The principal was fascinated by a report turned in by a little girl: "All the animals were funny. The best I liked was the Warning Stand Back. Every time we looked at it he spit at us."

Sister M. Annette, O.P.

SPACE RATES

A chimpanzee walked into a bar and ordered a cocktail. The bartender watched fascinated as the chimp sipped away in a leisurely fashion.

When he finished, the chimp laid a ten-dollar bill on the bar. The bartender took the ten dollars and slyly put down one dollar in change.

The chimp pocketed the money and was about to leave when the bartender remarked, "Sorry I looked so shocked when you came in, but we don't get many chimpanzees in here, you know."

"I'm sure you don't," returned the outraged customer. "Not when you charge nine dollars a drink!"

Spice Box.

NO FILTER

Victor Borge once felt called upon to explain why the keys of his own piano are yellow. "It's not really because the piano is old," he insisted. "It's just because the elephant smoked too much."

Philadelphia Inquirer.

DETERRENT TACTICS

"David, darling," a mother asked her small son, "why are you making faces at that bulldog?"

"Well," the child replied defensively, "he started it!"

E. McGowan.

PALS

Desegregation is moving ahead fast. Last week a bear was seen using a deer crossing.

Changing Times.

DOWN SAFE

A certain philosophical fish at the Philadelphia Aquarama was asked how he was getting along. "Oh, pretty fair," he replied. "At least I manage to keep my head below water."

Philadelphia Inquirer.

MUSTANGWAGEN

A city family were touring the barns of a farm when they saw a tiny colt. "Look, Daddy," the seven-year-old exclaimed, "a foreign horse."

Wall Street Journal.

AGONIZING REAPPRAISAL

A lion approached a rhinoceros and asked, "Who is the king of the jungle?" "You are, O lion," came the answer.

The lion went up to a hippopotamus and asked, "Who is the king of the jungle?" The hippo said, "You are, O lion."

The lion went up to an elephant and asked, "Who is the king of the jungle?" Whereupon the elephant seized the lion with his trunk, whirled him around, tossed him in the air, caught him on the way down, and slammed him into a tree.

Half-dazed, the lion shook himself and managed to mutter weakly, "Just because you don't know the right answer you don't have to get sore."

Quote.

MONKEY BUSINESS

In Kirby, Misperton, England, zoo officials paid out more than $280 to visitors last year for articles stolen from them by monkeys. The monkeys specialize in snatching eyeglasses from the wearers' noses as the visitors bend forward to make out a sign on the cage which reads: "Warning! These monkeys snatch glasses."

UPI.

THE NEW MATH AND THE OLD WORLD

Noah, after the flood subsided, opened the doors of the Ark and released the animals. All living creatures rushed to freedom, all, that is, except two snakes who lingered in a dark corner.

"Why don't you go forth and multiply?" Noah demanded in his sternest tones.

"We can't," one of the lengthy reptiles pointed out. "We're adders."

V.F.W. Magazine.

PSYCHIATRICKS

A mixed-up kangaroo went to see a psychiatrist. "I don't know what's the matter with me lately," he said, "but I just don't seem to be jumpy at all."

Harold Helfer.

FLIGHTS OF FANCY

Dog with a metronome tail—*Barnaby Conrad.*

Dog with a rag-rug pedigree—*Phyllis L. Strack.*

Penguins popping from the water like squeezed watermelon seeds—*Richard E. Byrd.*

Robin tug-o'-warring with a worm—*P. R. Engele.*

High up on the telephone pole human woodpeckers plied their trade—*J. K. Young.*

Taxis converged, eager as poodles called to supper—*Phyllis McGinley.*

Cocktail party: where people get together in staggering numbers—*John K. Young.*

VII THE THOUGHTS OF YOUTH

Illustration from *People Are Like That*

Kids Write What They Think

ૈ≈

BY H. ALLEN SMITH

Oliver Wendell Holmes once observed that children do pretty much all of the honest truth-telling there is in the world. H. Allen Smith supplies excellent proof in his latest book, provocatively titled *Don't Get Perconel with a Chicken*. The title comes from a postvacation essay by a young farm visitor who fell in love with a certain chicken only to see it served up on the dinner table. "When my gran father saw me crying he says dont ever get perconel with a chicken," she wrote. Here are some other samples of what Mr. Smith calls "nuggets from youthful pens."

The way some little boys pass the time is illustrated in an essay written by Dennis Heinemann of Los Angeles and passed along to posterity by Matt Weinstock: "A little boy was looking at his fish. They weren't doing anything so he went into his room and read a book. Some friends came over. They played records. Davy Crockett was their favorite. They played it two hundred times and then went to bed they were so tired."

Bruce Brill, another boy in Dennis' school, wrote an essay showing how jungle beasts pass the time: "Once there was a giraffe. He lived in the jungle. He liked to eat grass and bananas and leaves. At night he visited the other animals. They talked and played poker and drank lemonade until midnight."

This poker game fascinates me. I'd dearly love to see a giraffe drinking lemonade and worrying over his hole card.

A boy in New Jersey turned in the following bit of literary criticism:

Book Report
The book I report is Tarzan and the ant men. Their is no report because it would tell you how it turned out.

In my fat file of children's writings I have come upon a single sheet from a school composition book, with five words printed on it in large letters. The only identification is the name Stephen Sanborn, written on the back. The five words are:

WET PANT YOUS BAKE DOOR

Fred Beck is the authority for a story about a little girl who went to visit her aunt. The little girl had been raised in a heathen household, but her Aunt Elsie, a righteous woman, sent her to Sunday school. There she was given the first Sunday school card she had ever seen. She wrote home: "Dear Daddy: Aunt Elsie sent me to Sunday school and the kids sang hims and then they gave me an ad for heaven. love. Beatrice"

When Randy Jacob of Yardley, Pennsylvania, was eight years old his grandfather wanted the boy to develop an interest in nature. So he told Randy to go out and observe nature and write about it, and if the stuff he wrote was good, he would be given some money. Randy's first submission:

The spider is not an insect. It has 8 legs. Some people call it an insect when it is a plain bug. It is a pest to most people for it makes big cobwebs in corners of walls and other places and leaves it. Some people are even afraid of it.

The Yellowjacket is another stinging insect, it is a lot like the bee only smaller. It seems like it is meant for stinging because it has no other use. A bee makes honey, a wasp just walks around enjoying life, and hardly ever does any flying, but a yellowjacket seems to fly around stinging people on purpose.

Once, a book for children arrived at the New York *Herald Tribune* office. It was decided to hand it over to a twelve-year-old for review. The child wrote one of the shortest reviews on record, yet one of the most perceptive in the whole history of criticism—a commentary that could be applied to many another book: "This book is very good but too long in the middle."

Following publication of my book *Write Me a Poem, Baby*, some of my neighbors became more conscious of their children's writings than they had been in the past. One little girl was allowed to stay up election night and watch the excitement on TV. Afterward her mother suggested that she write her impressions of the election. She did. She wrote a poem.

> Clack clack
> Went the univac

When Johnnie Choate was nine years old he was given a writing assignment at school. He was told to read the English ballad *Lord Ullin's Daughter* and then to tell the story in his own words. Let us first have a look at what Johnnie wrote.

" 'Sandy' called Lord Ullin, Bring My daughter to me.' Yes Sire said Sandy. 'Come come my daughter I will take you to a castle wich we mite by.' 'O father you are always beying things. wy don't you think of the poor for a change.'
'O phhooy to the poor they should earn there money instead of beging for it.' "

'Father your so very crule.'

'Why daughter you speak souch bad talk.'

'It is very right what I say and speachy you saying boo to the poor. Why you ought to be a shamed of your shelf. Im going to run away.' "

That is as far as Johnnie went with it and I don't know what his teacher said if he turned it in. There is one small matter to be cleared up: that word *speachy*. After much soul-searching I decided that Johnnie meant "specially," and his mother verified my deduction.

Now, I was not acquainted with the original ballad and had to do some digging in the public library. One thing is certain: Johnnie didn't copy anything verbatim. In the ballad Lord Ullin's daughter and the chief of Ulva's Isle are eloping and have been on the road for three days, pursued by Lord Ullin and his men. At Lochgyle they plead with the ferryman to row them across. He agrees and Lord Ullin arrives on the shore just in time to see the boat capsize and his daughter drown.

That's all there is to it. Nobody named Sandy. No talk about castles to by. No *phhooy* to the poor. No daughter speaking souch bad talk. In fact, it appears to me that Johnnie was deeply dissatisfied with the whole plot of the ballad, even the elopement part.

When Cassy Espy was much younger than she is today, she decided to organize her affairs and lead an orderly existence. She went in for single-entry bookkeeping so that she might always know where she stood financially. Her mother has passed along a page from Cassy's account book, as follows:

$$
\begin{array}{lr}
\text{Candy} \ \dots\dots\dots\dots & 3 \\
\text{gum} \ \dots\dots\dots\dots\dots & 5 \\
\text{ribben} \ \dots\dots\dots\dots & 15 \\
\hline
\text{All toll} \ \dots\dots\dots & 23 \\
\end{array}
$$

One spring afternoon when she was about seven, Mona Espy was sitting in the yard. A sudden surge of religious feeling hit her. She hurried into the house, got pencil and paper, and wrote: "I Love you God I Love you so much that I wish that I was in the aire. to go. by mona."

Paul Nathan, who writes for *Publishers' Weekly*, served as one of the judges in a sixth-grade essay contest. All the children wrote on the subject "Courtesy, the Art of Being Nice." Mr. Nathan's favorite (though not the winner) was this one.

Courtesy can help us mentally, for it leaves us with a free conchonce & a happy soul. Courtesy has helped us win wars. Suppose the U.S. is being beaten in a war of missles by Russia. Briton chimes in & we soon beat Russia. They did this kind deed for they knew we could help them.

Courtesy can save money & lives too. Imagine that Ichabod is driving in the suburbs of a large establishment. Having smoked a cigar, he flicks it out the window. Ichabod's cigar started a gigantic fire which claimed 3,000,000 lives & just as many dollars damage. By the way, Ichabod's children were killed. He could have stopped this disaster by simply putting the cigar in the ashtray.

Another example . . . Say King Joe is visiting Mongolia. On his way he falls of a cliff, a phesant found him & cured him. In return, the king made the phesant a high official in his court. Also there is the story of the thorn in the lions paw & the boy gets it out so the lion repays him with his life. Courtesy Pays!!!

A Connecticut couple with a pair of eight-year-old twin girls named Carol and Clara allowed the children to spend a weekend at the country home of a couple who had no offspring. Clara appointed herself official chronicler of the expedition. She later presented the following report to her parents:

Mr. Fitzpatrick is deiting he wants to get skinny and look young. Carol gave me an Indin burn and I give her one back. They have an orgen and we practised on it it's easier than the piano. I would practice much on the orgen if we had one. They told us to look at the litning bugs and we did but we have litening bugs in Greenich but we don't look out. Mr. Fitzpatrick has a big gardon with corn but the corn is not as tall as our corn and dont grow as fast as our corn. They met in Masschuses Carol ask mr. Fizpatrick who proposed to who and he said mrs. Fizpatrick proposed to him but mrs. Fizpatrick said he was a fibre and dont believe a word he says. They drunk ten cans of beer. They have 2 bird feders but not as nice as ours and the skwerels get on them.

Laurette Howars once published a collection of children's things. It included a marvelous essay.

Smells

Smells are things to know about. When people do good things they smell sweet. When they do bad things, they do not smell sweet at all. Dogs know about this.

An equally perceptive essay, written by a schoolgirl, was reprinted by the Boston *Evening Transcript.* It bore the title "Parents":

"We get our parents at so late an age that it is impossible to change their habits."

CHANGING LYRICS

I did a double take when I heard the neighborhood kids singing Christmas carols outside our house one crisp night in December. It couldn't be, I thought, but I listened carefully, and sure enough, I heard: "As shepherds washed their socks by night. . . ."

J. C.

The kindergartner proudly reported to her parents that the class had learned Irving Berlin's "God Bless America." Then she proceeded to sing:

> God bless America, land that I love;
> Stand beside her and guide her,
> Through the night with a light from a bulb.
>
> *Mrs. Deane Binder.*

PEOPLE ARE LIKE THAT

Once while shopping at the local florist's I became fascinated by the behavior of three not quite teen-age boys. They were sporting gloves and oddly assorted uniforms and I gathered that they had just come from playing baseball.

They blushed and stuttered when the young lady in charge asked what they wanted. It seemed that they were in the market for a corsage. The girl inquired whether it was to be for a young or old person, and what variety of flowers did they have in mind? Three puzzled heads went together and there was a great deal of debating and counting of coins from various pockets.

"Would $4.32 buy a couple of orchids?" one of them asked.

"Orchids!" The clerk's eyebrows flew up in astonishment. "Something very special, I take it?"

"You know old Mrs. Murphy, down at Park Street? Well, she let us play ball in her field all summer. Now school is going to open and we took up a collection to have a party. Only none of our mothers wants twelve boys in the house at once—none of 'em. But Mrs. Murphy said that next sodality night, while she was gone, we could have the party in her house if we behaved and did the cleaning up after. That's why we got to get her some orchids—to sort of say 'Thank you.' "

The clerk suggested a potted plant or some cut flowers, but the boys would not be put off. She finally put a special price of $4.32 on two orchids, made up into a corsage and delivered with a suitable card. After the delighted committee counted out the sum, they had a bit less than $1.50 left over for refreshments.

A friend in the sodality told me later that old Mrs. Murphy simply sailed down the aisle in her orchids that Tuesday night.

Ruth Dillon Kiniry.

QUIZ KID

My precocious niece, age five, loves to fill in blanks in newspapers. Here are some of her responses to a quiz entitled "Which Side?"

On which side do you mount a horse? *top side*

On which side do you button a man's coat? *out side.*

On which side does a United States driver sit when he drives a car? *in side*

Mrs. William Graybill in Coronet.

ORCHIDS TO US

A housewife was so pleased with the promptness shown by the grocer's delivery boy that she asked him his name.

"Bill Shakespeare," replied the boy.

"Well, that's quite a famous name!" laughed the housewife.

"It should be," replied the boy promptly. "I've been delivering in this neighborhood for almost three years now."

Scholastic Teacher.

EASY MONEY

Two eight-year-old boys in my neighborhood offered to wash my car for 10¢ apiece. I told them to go ahead, and then paid them no further attention. When they came to collect, I asked them how business was going.

"Oh, fine!" one of them replied. "Mr. Brown over across the street walked over to watch us—and he gave us each a quarter *not* to wash his car."

Clarence Roeser.

WATCH THE BIRDIE!

One of my neighbor's sons was to march in the Memorial Day parade in our town. My neighbor, armed with a camera, took up a position along the parade route. As his boy came marching by, the father aimed his camera, then tried to get the lad's attention. But the ranks stepped on, eyes straight ahead.

An attractive teen-ager, sizing up the situation, yelled, "Hey, handsome!" Every GI turned his head toward her—and the proud father got his picture.

Mrs. S. Lee.

GOOD TO THE LAST CRUMB

Bobby was just finishing the cake as his mother stepped into the kitchen.

"Why, Bobby," she remonstrated, "you ate all the cake without even thinking of your little sister!"

"No I didn't!" replied Bobby. "I was thinking of her all the time. I was afraid she'd get here before I finished."

Gottfried von Kronenberger.

POWER OF PRAYER

At a mission in Idaho I was collecting children to drive them to catechism class when I came upon a girl arguing loftily with her little three-year-old brother. "No, Fatty," she said, "you aren't big enough to come. You don't even know your prayers."

157

Fatty was furious. "You ole smarty!" he shouted. "I do too know my prayers!" He snatched up a handful of rocks and started reciting. "Hail Mary, full of grace!" he shouted, and a rock whistled past his sister. "The Lord is with thee . . ." and another rock. We drove swiftly away, but I heard him still shouting, "Holy Mary!" as the last rock bounced off my rear bumper.

Mrs. May Gumm.

HIS FATHER'S CHILD

While the child psychologist tinkered with his car, his small son played with the girl next door. Suddenly the boy gave his playmate a violent push and she fell to the ground.

Before the astonished father could begin to scold, the youngster turned to him and asked innocently, "Daddy, why did I do that?"

Wall Street Journal.

WAY OUT

Three beatniks were driving along, doing about ninety, when the one in the back seat noticed that his door was rattling and slammed it shut.

The driver glanced suspiciously at the mirror. "Hey, man," he asked, "who got in?"

S. J. Gudge.

A-1 TERRITORY

A man who sells advertising space for a metropolitan newspaper had never been able to figure out the deferential attitude all the children of his suburban block seemed to have toward him.

One recent evening he came upon a cluster of small boys, who all fell silent when he stopped to say hello. Then one of the lads blurted, "Are you really a *space salesman?*"

Frances Benson.

THESE TWAIN

Not long ago my office nurse, an attractive single girl, gave me her usual morning greeting and held out an open box of cigars. (I'd already heard that she had been proffering them to the other male members of the clinic staff, too.)

"Thank you, that's very thoughtful, but is there any particular occasion?" I asked.

She extended her left hand and I saw a sparkling diamond on the third finger. "It's a boy!" she announced. "Six feet, dark, one hundred and eighty-five pounds."

Dr. L. Binder.

CERREALISM

A five-year-old I know likes to play mother to her two younger sisters. One morning, as the three girls were having breakfast, the two younger ones seemed to be dawdling.

"Eat your toast; it's getting cold," said the eldest sternly to one of them. "And you," she went on, turning to the other, "eat your cereal! It's almost quiet."

C. Kennedy.

A TASTE FOR HONEY

I was watching our little Jimmy as he walked down the street, heading for his first day at school. To my horror I saw a huge

159

dog come bounding out of my neighbor's yard and make straight for Jimmy.

The dog leaped on him and Jimmy, a timid soul, began to scream. I raced to the scene only to find to my relief that the dog was joyfully licking Jimmy's face. But Jimmy continued to howl.

"The dog didn't bite you, did he?" I asked.

"No," sobbed Jimmy. "But he tasted me."

Florence V. Bradish.

WESTERNS

As one little fourth grader handed in his drawing lesson, Sister exclaimed, "Why, Johnny, this looks as if that cowboy is going into a saloon!"

"He is, Sister," the boy replied. "But it's OK. He's not going to drink anything. He's only going to shoot a guy."

Charles Chick Govin.

AGE

To keep her youth a girl should not introduce him to her friends.

D. H.

FIRST THINGS FIRST

A neighbor of ours was idly watching seven or eight small children playing hide-and-seek. The game went smoothly for a while, but then a problem arose.

The smallest boy, barely three, was "it," and he couldn't count to one hundred. In fact he couldn't even count to ten with

160

any consistency. How were the others going to get enough time to hide properly if the "it" boy couldn't count?

The gang went into a huddle. Then a little girl about six, obviously a real brain, figured out a solution and issued instructions to the tiny boy.

So, while the other kids scattered and hid, the little boy turned his back, covered his eyes, and recited the Our Father.

John Maguire in the Albany Times-Union.

DISENGAGEMENT

First grader Melanie had announced that she was engaged to marry the young gentleman next door, but the engagement was broken abruptly.

"Why aren't you going to marry Danny?" asked Melanie's mother.

"Well," replied the child loftily, "he just isn't ready for marriage yet. And besides that," she added, "he scribbled in my coloring book."

C. Kennedy.

PENANCE IN PRINT

There was a little girl in the beauty salon the other day, waiting for her mother. Someone handed her, of all things, a *True Confessions* magazine to help her while away the time.

The little girl looked at the title and asked, "How did you know I was Catholic?"

Madeleine Dunlay.

ALL IN THE FAMILY

The other day our second grade teacher was registering two little boys who were transferring from another school. She

161

noticed their surnames were the same and that they were about the same size and dressed alike, so she asked, "Are you twins?"

"No," one of them replied.

Then she read the birth dates on their transfer slips and there was only about six months difference in their ages. So she asked, "Are you cousins?"

"No," said the other boy, "we're brothers."

"Well, I think," said the teacher, "that there must be some mistake here in the dates of your birth. Will you please have your mother write down when each of you was born and bring it to me tomorrow?"

"Why?" asked one of the boys.

"Because," explained the teacher, "if you aren't twins and you are brothers, George would have to be more than six months older than Larry."

The boys looked at each other. Then George turned to the teacher with a smile and said, "But I don't have to be more older, 'cause you see one of us is adopted. But I don't know which one."

Lois Koch.

CHILDREN'S BRIGHT-EYED VIEW OF LIFE

"A tickle is you laugh."

"A spanking is if you won't speak to them, they'll give you another one."

These are some first graders' definitions, dictated to teacher Mrs. Judith Hudson at Salt Lake City's McKinley School. They illustrate not only that children get to the heart of things, but that some are poets.

"A smile is what happens when you help somebody," said Mike Blackwell, six.

If you couldn't tell Maile Hutchings was a girl from her name, you could from her comment: "Eyelashes are so boys think you look cute."

Tracy Byington said, "A grandmother is an old mother." But Brad Codery disagreed. "A grandma," he said, "is to cook eggs."

Some others: "A snowman is to melt in the sun." "A mustache is you have them on your chin." And the school principal? "A principal owns the traffic patrol."

AP

TELEPHONE GRAMMAR

When my college-aged daughter answered the phone, an unfamiliar male voice said, "Come on over, we're waiting for you."

Much annoyed, she inquired, "To whom do you wish to speak?"

There was a long pause, and then the man replied "I'm sorry! I must have the wrong number. Nobody I know says 'whom.' "

Mrs. D. Binder.

TAKE-HOME PAY

A little boy decided he wanted $100, so he also decided to pray for it. Unsuccessful, he wrote to God. The post office forwarded the letter to the White House and the President ordered that $4 be sent to the boy.

Delighted that his prayers had been at least partially answered, the lad wrote a thank-you note to God, adding, "I notice you routed my letter through Washington and as usual they deducted 95%."

Vera Ferris.

INTEGRATION

Gail entered a Catholic school that had several Negro families. At dinner the first night her mother asked, "Are there any colored children in your class?"

"What color?" Gail wanted to know.

Lois M. Robillard.

LITURGICAL ACROBATS

Little Terry's grandmother was taking him to Mass for the first time. As they entered the church she whispered to him, "Do you know how to genuflect?"

"No," he whispered back. "But I know how to somersault."

Gladys Kent.

COEDUCATION

High-school girl to teen-age friend: "I wrote to sixteen colleges and this one had the best rating: 1,479 boys and 215 girls."

Frances Benson.

PRIORITY

An enchanting little girl of eight received a phone call from a schoolmate. "Please call me back in ten minutes," she requested, "I'm in the middle of a tantrum."

C. Kennedy.

FLIGHTS OF FANCY

When a closed mind reopens, it's usually under the same old management—*Caroline Clark.*

164

The best test of manners is how to put up with bad ones—The
   Furrow.
Perseverence: stubbornness put to good use—Wall Street
   Journal.
Diplomacy: lying in state—*Mary Singleton.*
Inflation: the system whereby if you save up long enough to
   buy something you can't afford it—*Charles Chick Govin.*
Potential oil well: a site to be holed—Advertising Age.
Quadruplets: four crying out loud—Straight.

VIII EXAMINATION AND CONFESSION

Illustration from *Women Want to Know Everything*

Women Are Better Drivers

ౘ≫

BY PHYLLIS McGINLEY

That men are wonderful is a proposition I will defend to the death. Honest, intrepid, talented, strong, and handsome, they are my favorite gender. Consider the things men can do better than women: mend the plumbing, cook, invent atom bombs, design the Empire waistline, and run the four-minute mile. They can throw a ball overhand. They can grow a beard.

I can think of only two accomplishments at which women excel. Having babies is one. The other is driving an automobile.

Don't misunderstand me. Some of my best friends are male drivers. They seldom go to sleep at the wheel or drive ninety on a forty-five-an-hour road or commit any other of the sins of which statistics accuse them. But insurance companies have been busy as bees proving that I don't get around among the right people.

In New York State, where I live, they have even made it expensive to have sons. Car insurance costs much more if there are men in the family under twenty-five driving than if there are only women. Obviously the females of the species make the better chauffeurs.

They ought to. They get the most practice. Aside from truck and taxi drivers, it is women who really handle the cars of the nation. Five days of the week they are slipping cleverly through traffic on their thousand errands: parking neatly in front of chain stores, ferrying their husbands to and from commuting trains, and driving the young to schools and dentists and dancing classes and Scout meetings. It is only on Saturdays and Sundays that men get their innings, not to speak of their outings, and it is over weekends when most of the traffic catastrophes occur.

Not that men are responsible for all the accidents. Some are caused by women—by the little blond on the sidewalk at whom the male driver feels impelled to whistle; or by the pretty girl sitting in the front seat for whom he wants to show off his skill, his eagle eye, and the way he can pull ahead of that red Jaguar.

But it isn't caution and practice alone which make the difference. It's chiefly an attitude of mind. Women, in my opinion, are the practical ones. To us a car is a means of transportation. It is a gadget more complicated, perhaps, than a dishwasher or a can opener, but no more romantic. It is something in which we can carry the sheets to the laundry, pick up Johnnie at kindergarten, and lug home rosebushes.

Men, the dear, sentimental creatures, feel otherwise. To them automobiles are more than means of transportation. They are their shining chariots, the objects of their affections. A good man loves his car the way the Lone Ranger loves his horse, and he feels for its honor on the road. No one must get off to a better jackrabbit start. And no one, but no one, must tell him anything while he's driving. My own husband, ordinarily the most good-tempered of men, becomes a tyrant behind the wheel.

"Shouldn't we bear south here?" I inquire meekly on our

Saturday trips to the country; or, "Honey, there's a gray convertible trying to pass."

"Who's driving?" he snarls like Simon Legree, veering stubbornly north or avoiding, by a hair, being run into.

Women drivers, on the other hand, take advice. They are used to taking it, having had it pressed on them all their lives by their mothers, teachers, beaux, husband, and eventually their children. And when they don't know their route exactly, they inquire at service stations, from passersby, from traffic officers. But men hate to ask and when they are forced to do so, seldom listen.

Have you ever overheard a woman taking down directions on the phone? "Yes," she may say affably. "I understand. I drive up that pretty road to the Danbury turnoff. Then I bear left at the little antique shop that used to be a barn—yellow with blue shutters. Then right at a meadow with two beech trees in it, and a couple of black cows. Up a little lane, just a tiny way beyond a cornfield, and that's your place. Yes. With a Tiffany-glass carriage lamp in front. Fine. I won't have any trouble." Nor does she.

A man has too much pride to take such precautions. "OK," he says impatiently. "Two point seven miles off the Post Road. A left, a rotary, another left. Six point three to—oh, never mind. I'll check the map."

When they don't insist on traveling by ear, men travel by chart. I've nothing against road maps, really, except the way they clutter up the glove compartment, where I like to keep tissues and sunglasses. But men have a furtive passion for them.

When my husband and I are planning a trip, he doesn't rush out like me to buy luggage and a new wardrobe. He shops for maps. For days ahead of time he studies them dotingly; then I am forced to study them en route. Many a bitter journey have I taken past the finest scenery in America with my eyes glued to a collection of black and red squiggles on a road map, instead of on the forests and canyons we had come all the way across the country to behold.

"Look!" I cry to him as we rush up some burning autumn lane. "Aren't the trees glorious?"

"What does the map say?" he mutters. "I've marked a covered bridge about a quarter of a mile along here. That's where we turn."

If we should ever approach the Pearly Gates together, I know exactly how the conversation will run. "See all the pretty stars," I'll be murmuring happily. "And, oh, do look over there! Isn't that the City of Gold?"

"Never mind your golden cities," he'll warn me sternly as he nearly collides with a meteor. "Just keep your eye on the map."

Women Want to Know Everything

ह↬

BY PARKE CUMMINGS

A woman's curiosity is too darned hard to satisfy, no matter how desperately her husband strives to fill her in on what she wants to know. The other night was a perfect case in point.

I play in a weekly stag bridge game with Joe, Sam, and Hank in which we rotate among homes. The night in question it was my turn to entertain, but Joe couldn't play. He procured a substitute, a man I hadn't met before.

When he came in the door, Virginia, my wife, caught a brief glimpse of him before we turned out of the front hall and headed for the bridge table in my downstairs study.

We had a brisk game winding up at 12:42 A.M. The next morning Virginia asked me about our new guest.

"What's his name?" she inquired.

"Bill," I told her.

"Bill who?"

"I don't think I got his last name," I confessed. "When I kept score I just marked him down as Bill. He ended up a dollar thirty-five to the good, I recall."

"What's he like?" she pursued.

"Well," I said, "he's a little inclined to overbid, but he's a very shrewd defensive player. One time he set me on what seemed a sure contract by trumping his partner's ace. Ordinarily this would be a bonehead play, but he did it deliberately. It enabled him to lead back a club and trap my king in dummy. Another time—"

"No, no," she broke in, "I mean what sort of a person is he? Is he the intellectual type, the hard-boiled type, or—"

"I'd say a combination of both. He certainly showed a high degree of intelligence the way he played that redoubled slam in hearts. He did it by putting a squeeze on Hank. On the other hand, he's plenty hard-boiled. A couple of hands later I accidentally reneged and he insisted on exacting a two-trick penalty. Of course, he had every right to because the rule specifically says—"

"What does he do?" she said.

I scratched my head. "Search me," I said.

"You were with him for over four hours and you haven't the faintest idea whether he's a banker or a beekeeper or—"

"Wait a minute," I broke in. "That last gives me a clue. He wouldn't be likely to be a beekeeper—he works in the city."

"How did you glean that bit of information?" she asked sweetly.

"Because I now recall that he commutes on the eight eleven and plays bridge in the smoking car. Yesterday he had the most fantastic hand. Eight spades to the ace, king, queen, ten, nine, *no* clubs, *no* diamonds, and five hearts to the king, queen, jack, ten. So he bids—"

"Is he married?" she inquired.

"Yep," I answered. "I remember his remarking that his wife simply cannot play no-trump hands. Insist on playing all her high cards first, thereby setting up tricks for the opponents."

"Wonderful!" Virginia acknowledged. "I feel as though I'd known her all my life. Children?"

"Children," I mused, "children. Let's see now. Yes, they must have. He was complaining that one of his kids got hold of a brand-new deck of cards and messed them all up with crayons."

"How does he stand politically?" Virginia demanded.

"Pretty hard to say," I told her. "He seems to consider Eisenhower a first-rate bridge player, but he put in a good word for a couple of Democratic senators. I can't recall who they were, offhand; they use the Goren two-bid with—"

"Go no further," interrupted my better half. "I feel I know everything about him that there is to know. It's simply uncanny what a keen interest you take in people as people. You meet a total stranger and within a few hours you discover every last detail about him."

"Thanks," I said modestly.

The Ten Worst Things About a Man

ε❧

BY JEAN KERR

I feel a bit of a fraud to be picking on men, since I always pretend to be so crazy about them. And, deep down inside, I *am* crazy about them. They are sweet, you know, and so helpful.

At parties men you've barely met will go back to the buffet to get you a muffin, and they will leap to their feet to tell you that you've got the wrong end of the cigarette in your mouth. When you are trying to squeeze into a tight parking place, there will always be some nice man driving by who will shout, "Lady, you've got a whole *mile* back there!"

But, charming as men are, we can't pretend they're perfect. It wouldn't be good for them and it wouldn't be true. Marrying a man is like buying something you've been admiring for a long time in a shop window. You may love it when you get it home, but it doesn't always go with everything else in the house.

176

One reason is that most men behave as though this were an orderly sensible universe. That naturally makes them hard to live with. The other reason they're hard to live with (I know this sounds illogical) is that they're so *good*. Here are a few of their more intolerable virtues.

1. *A man will not meddle in his wife's affairs.* He may interfere at the office, driving secretaries to drink and premature marriage by snooping in file drawers and tinkering with the mimeograph machine. But, once back home in the nest, he is the very model of *laissez-faire.* He will stare at you across the dining-room table (as you simultaneously carve the lamb and feed the baby) and announce, in tones so piteous as to suggest that all his dreams have become ashes, "There's no salt in this shaker." What a wife objects to is not just that daddy has lived in this house for thirteen years without ever discovering where the salt is kept. It's more the implication that only she has the fortitude, stamina, and simple animal cunning necessary to pour the salt into that little hole in the shaker.

2. *A man remembers important things.* It really is remarkable the fund of information he keeps at his fingertips: the date of the Battle of Hastings, the name of the man who invented the printing press, the formula for water, the preamble to the Constitution, and every lyric Larry Hart ever wrote. It is unreasonable to expect one so weighted down with relevant data to remember what size shirt he takes, or what grade Gilbert is in, or even what you told him fifteen times.

A woman just has to go through life remembering for two. I know one wife who occasionally pins a tag on her husband's overcoat. The tag reads, "Please don't give me a ride home from the station. I have my own car today." However, this technique wouldn't work with my husband. He usually leaves his overcoat on the train.

3. *A man will try to improve your mind.* Working on the

suspicion that women read nothing in the newspaper except bulletins from Macy's and Dorothy Kilgallen, the average man takes considerable pains to keep his scatterbrained wife *au courant* with the contemporary political situation. And we get the following dialogue in consequence.

"Did you read Walter Lippmann today on the shake-up in the Defense Department?"

"No. What did he have to say?"

"You should have read it. It was an excellent piece."

"Well, what was the gist of it?"

"Where is that paper? It should be around here someplace."

"It's not around here someplace. It went out with the garbage."

"That's too bad. It would have clarified the whole situation for you."

"I'm sure. But what was he saying?"

"Oh, he was talking about the shake-up in the Defense Department."

"I know that, but what did he *say?*"

"He was against it."

4. *A man allows you to make the important decisions.* Because he has such respect for your technical know-how, he is constantly asking questions like "Does this kid need a sweater?" or "Is that baby wet?" Personally I am willing to go through life being the court of last appeal on such crucial issues as bedtime (is it?), cookies (can he have another?), rubbers (do they have to wear them?), and baths (tonight? but they took one last night). But just between us, I have no confidence in a man who wanders to the kitchen, peers into the icebox, and asks plaintively, "Do I want a sandwich?"

5. *A man will give you an honest answer.* If you say, "Honey, do you think this dress is too tight for me to wear?" he will say, "Boy, it sure is!"

6. *A man takes pride in his personal possessions.* A wife usually cherishes the belief that her husband would give her the shirt off his back. Thus she is in no way prepared for his cries of outrage should she ever be rash enough to *take* the shirt off his back. It doesn't matter that the shirt in question has a torn pocket and a frayed collar, and has, in any case, been at the bottom of the clothes hamper for four years. It's his, and you wear it at your risk.

My husband will say to me, "What are you doing in that shirt, for heaven's sake?" Now, he doesn't really want to know what I'm doing. He can see what I'm doing. I'm painting the garage doors. He just wants me to know that his shirt is near and dear to him.

There are two possible solutions to this problem. You can hire a painter to paint the garage doors, or you can dye the shirt purple so your husband won't be able to recognize it.

7. *A man believes in sharing.* Men are all advocates of Togetherness, up to a point. They will agree that it is "our house," "our mortgage," and, of course, "our song." However, some items that once were "our" joint concern suddenly become your exclusive possession. For instance, a man will return from a stroll through "our back yard" to tell you, "Honey, I think your daffodils are getting clump-bound." Or he will say, "I see that the hinge is off your medicine chest." This policy of dissociating from anything that is temporarily out of order reaches its ultimate confusion with statements like "Hey, your man is here to fix the chimney." My man? I never saw him before in my life.

8. *A man doesn't want you to worry.* Since he supposes, quite correctly, that you worry about his health, he tries to spare you alarm about his physical condition. He will say casually, "Well, I almost keeled over in Grand Central today."

"Heavens!" you will say, "What happened?"

"Nothing, nothing. I leaned against a pillar. I didn't fall down."

"But, honey, what happened? Did you feel faint? You didn't have a terribly sharp pain in your chest, did you?"

"Oh, no. No, nothing like that."

"Well, what do you mean you almost keeled over?"

"I almost keeled over, that's all."

"But there must have been some *reason*."

"Oh, I guess it's that foot again."

"What foot again? Which foot?"

"The one that's been numb since last summer."

"Your foot has been numb since last summer?"

"Now it's more like the whole leg."

"Well then, let's call the doctor. Let's call this minute!"

"Why?"

"Why? Are you out of your mind? Because there's something the matter with your leg, that's why!"

"See, there you go, flying off again. I'm sorry I mentioned it. There's nothing the matter with my leg, nothing."

9. *A man is reasonable.* There is nothing wrong with a man's being reasonable as long as he doesn't insist on your being reasonable, too. "Let's be *reasonable*," he keeps saying, about as often as he says, "Go ask your mother" and "What's for dinner?" The occasions on which he thinks you should be reasonable vary. But it's usually any time you're driven past your endurance by shiftless department stores (who promised faithfully to deliver that crib three weeks ago) and irresponsible cleaning women (who simply don't show up on the day you're having sixteen guests to dinner).

At times like these a woman wishes only a word of sympathy, like "Yes, yes, they're all a bad lot." Any man who urges his wife to consider the possibility that Hattie really *has* "the virus" deserves to wax the floors himself.

10. *A man idealizes his wife.* This is another way of saying

that he hasn't really looked at her in fourteen years. To get me a housecoat for my birthday my husband will make the unthinkable sacrifice of entering Lord & Taylor's and even penetrating the awesome portals of the lingerie department. There he selects the slimmest, trimmest little salesgirl on the floor and announces, "She's about your size." Naturally I have to take the thing back and get myself a housecoat four sizes larger.

But, I shouldn't complain about that. If you stop and think, it's really rather charming of him.

MOMENT OF TRUTH

"Do you have trouble making up your mind?" inquired the psychiatrist.

"Well, yes and no," replied the patient.

Albany Times-Union.

HOW TRUE

The best way to wipe out a friendship is to sponge on it.

S. J. Gudge.

The wife who can read her husband like a book is usually a critic.

Francis O'Walsh.

The first Ten Commandments are the hardest.

Dan Bennett.

All the Constitution guarantees is the pursuit of happiness. You have to catch up with it yourself.

Benjamin Franklin.

FROM THE COUCH

A man complained to his psychiatrist that he was having trouble remembering things.

"What kind of things?" asked the psychiatrist.

"Oh, just anything at all—the date, what I had for breakfast, where I left my laundry. You name it and I forget it," replied the patient.

"How long has this been going on?" was the psychiatrist's next question.

"How long has what been going on?" inquired the patient.

G. R.

DEEP THERAPY

At the conclusion of a lengthy interview the psychiatrist told his patient to walk over to the window and stick out his tongue.

"Why?" inquired the patient, to whom this seemed a rather strange request.

"Because," replied the doctor, "I don't like that other psychiatrist over there across the court."

Pageant.

THAT'S LIFE

Everybody talks about getting old, and everybody is doing something about it, too.

Ida Tiritilli.

PSYCHIATRICKS

My neighbor is always boasting about her son, who is a self-made success. "He has a fine apartment on Park Avenue; his shoes are imported from Italy; he wears one hundred and fifty dollar suits made to his order," she was going on. "Why, even when he goes to the doctor, he pays him twenty-five dollars a visit just to talk to him while he rests on a couch."

"You mean twenty-five dollars for just one visit—just to talk?" I asked, trying to appear very impressed. "What does he talk about?"

The woman blushed prettily and flashed me a look of even greater pride. "Me," she said simply.

Mrs. Deane Binder.

BEWARE!

Driving on the superhighway is rather like playing Russian roulette. You never know which driver is loaded.

Philadelphia Inquirer.

TEMPERANCE, PLEASE

We were attending a cocktail party, when one of the guests turned to her husband and remarked severely, "Eddie, don't you dare take another drink! Your face is already getting blurred."

Mrs. Deane Binder.

POUNDS OF SIN

At an Altar and Rosary meeting some ladies were discussing dieting. "Father," one asked, "can breaking a diet ever be a sin?"

"Breaking one your doctor ordered might be," Father answered. "But it's not normally a sin. We're all temples of the Holy Spirit. If you want to be a basilica it's up to you."

Sister Mary Henrietta.

FLIGHTS OF FANCY

Even when he's alone, he's in bad company.—*"Barbs."*

Cash: the poor man's credit card.—*Fletcher Knebel.*

Even if you are on the right track, you will get run over if you just sit there.—*M. Dale Baughman.*

Sentimentality: sentiment we don't share.—*Graham Greene.*

A narrow-minded man can look through a keyhole with both eyes.—*St. Paul* Pioneer Press.

Sympathy: your pain in my heart—*H. E. Luccock.*

Walks with a southern drawl—*Mary Phyllis Riedley.*

IX FAMILY CIRCLE

Illustration from *Computer Cussedness*

Pope John Today

ह्र

BY FRANCIS SUGRUE

Cardinal Canali spoke from the balcony of St. Peter's at six o'clock on the evening of October 28, 1958: "I announce to you a great joy. We have a Pope: the most Eminent and Reverend Lord Cardinal Roncalli, who has chosen the name of John the twenty-third."

The multitude gave the dramatic announcement its time-honored reception; but when the tumult and shouting had died, many people began to ask, "Who is he?" To be sure, Cardinal Roncalli was known in diplomatic circles. For thirty years he had been a papal representative, first in Bulgaria, then in Turkey and Greece, finally in Paris. He had been the popular Patriarch of Venice for five years. But before the election newspaper stories speculating on the next Pope had his name in the last paragraph if he were mentioned in the papers at all.

It wasn't long before the new Pope's benevolent countenance was recognized by everyone. People felt the warmth of his character just by looking at his pictures. Some started calling him Uncle John. A news magazine said he was becoming the best-loved Pope of modern times. Cardinal Cushing of Boston called him "Good Pope John."

Like good wine he has warmed the imagination of people living in a cold, tasteless world. Stories about him have delighted Catholics and non-Catholics alike.

In the week before his coronation an aide asked a question, expecting a command. "Ask me some other time," Pope John said. "I am not broken in yet."

In addressing a Pope one is supposed to use the title "Most Blessed Father." In the early days of his pontificate every time he heard the salutation John turned in surprise.

According to tradition, Catholics kneel when they enter and when they leave the presence of the Holy Father.

John didn't mind occasional visitors doing that, but when his aides went to their knees at every coming and going he saw fit to take drastic action.

Word was passed that members of the Vatican staff were to kneel twice a day, once on greeting him in the morning and once before saying good-night.

He began turning up in unexpected places. Because he had relished a meal prepared for seminarians from forty countries visiting Castel Gandolfo, he went into the kitchen to thank the cooks. He told them how he had once tried his hand at cooking, but without marked success.

"My mother told me to watch the cornmeal mush and take it off when it boiled," he said. "I did. I took it off as soon as the first bubble appeared. It was a disaster."

When Cardinal Roncalli became Pope John, his valet, Guido Gusso, who had served him for many years, found it difficult to cope with the fact that his master was now the representative of Christ on earth. When called he would rush to the Pope and fall at once on his knees. He had trouble coming to his feet again even when the Pope said sharply, "Get off your knees." John considered it an unseemly way for a man to carry on before a former peasant.

"Forgive me, but it is stronger than I," Guido tried to explain. He said that a mysterious force kept pushing him down in the Pope's presence.

"If you go on behaving like this," John grumbled, "I'll have to look for another valet. Let's pretend that we are still in Venice."

The custom of the Pope's eating alone was contrary to John's nature. As nuncio to Paris he had a maxim that a good table and a good cellar are great assets in the art of diplomacy. In Venice he kept an open house, explaining that at any time someone might wander in who was hungry, or "might even go to Confession."

"They want me to eat by myself," Pope John lamented. But this crisis he dissolved in record time. "I tried it for one week and I was not comfortable," he said. "Then I searched through Sacred Scripture for something saying I had to eat alone. I found nothing, so I gave it up and it's much better now."

His coronation was on November 4, 1958. Afterward he sat down to table in his Vatican apartment with his sister and three brothers, who still lived in or around Sotto Il Monte, the village where the Pope was born. Also on hand for the meal were eighteen nephews, nieces, and cousins, who sat at a table in the next room. They enjoyed a blithe few hours of chatting, laughing, and dining. The scene would have made an interesting painting.

The Pope's sister, Assunta, seventy-three, had arrived at the Vatican carrying a large supply of homemade sausage. It was all for her brother, she said, because "God knows what kind of food they give him here." The brothers, Saverio, Alfredo, and Giuseppe, were weighed down with heavy cardboard suitcases. "We have been told that city food is not as good as ours."

The custom of the Pope's eating alone did have a common-sense basis. In this way His Holiness wouldn't run the risk of offending anyone. If he ate with one cardinal, wouldn't he have to give every member of the Sacred College a turn? If he asked the head of one state to stay for lunch, would it not be considered a snub to another nation if its chief of state was not invited?

The papal advisers had some bad moments when the Queen Mother and Princess Margaret called on the Pope in April, 1959. He wished to serve them lunch. "No, no," the advisers said, hoping the Pope wouldn't insist. He finally was persuaded that his proposed lunch might be too much of a shock for Vatican precedent.

The Holy Father just cannot abide formality when it comes to refreshment time. For him, drinking a cup of tea or a glass of wine with company is a practical expression of God's command to love one another. Returning from an audience one day, he found upholsterers at work in his apartment. He invited them to lunch. The men protested in horror that they could not think of doing such a thing; the very idea of eating with the Pope seemed sacrilegious. So John made arrangements for them to eat in the adjoining room.

The day after his election the new Pope made a tour of his territory. No Pontiff in at least forty years had inspected the Vatican so thoroughly.

It has taken time for the nine-hundred-odd Vatican citizens to get used to the gregarious Pope John. He wants to know about everything as he follows his rule of "seeing much" and correcting "just a little."

One thing he corrected was the wage scale of Vatican employees. They would have been considered low in almost any part of Italy. To be sure, the Vatican people did pay low rents and had the right to buy in a tax-free grocery and pharmacy, but still they had to scrimp with a pay envelope that sometimes contained $20 a week. John thinks that a Church which preaches social justice should set an example by paying its help well.

When one of his assistants asked him when he wanted the roof of St. Peter's closed off, the Pope didn't comprehend. It was explained that the roof is open to tourists except when the Pope takes his walk in the Vatican Gardens.

"Let the roof stay open while I'm out," John said. "I promise not to give any scandal to tourists."

Pope John usually retires at nine or ten o'clock at night. After a few hours of sleep he may get out of bed to work an hour or two in his study. Yet he is up again at 4 A.M. to begin the day's work. At the Vatican it is said, "He is like the country curate who awakens the town by ringing the church bell. The first one up in the Vatican every day is the Pope."

People who have an audience with him say they come away from the experience filled with a rare gladness. Pius XII inspired awe when he was first seen and then respect often turned to affection. John immediately brings to mind a jovial, kindly friend of the family.

One audience was a particularly happy occasion for the Pope as well as for his visitors. Fifty gondoliers from Venice came to Rome. He said the sight of them made him long to see the city of canals once again. They gave him a glass gondola.

Another time Pope John granted an audience to a circus troupe of 250 animal tamers, riders, clowns, and acrobats. The Pope patted Dolly, a playful lion cub, and reminded the animal, "You must behave here. We are only used to the calm lion of Saint Mark" (a reference to the lion in the papal coat of arms). The owners offered to leave the lion with the Pope, but his assistants hastily refused the gift before he could answer.

In most of his audiences he speaks Italian, but he is fluent, in varying degrees, in other languages, too. He terms his French *comme çi, comme ça* (so-so). One French visitor said, after a papal audience, "John is the only person in Italy who admits to speaking French imperfectly. And it isn't true. His French is fine." The Holy Father also speaks Bulgarian, Turkish, and modern Greek. He understands a bit of Russian, too.

When the Queen Mother and Princess Margaret called on him, the conversation was in French. John apologized for not speaking English; he promised the royal ladies that "it will be the next language I learn." He told Cardinal Spellman that someday he would master the English language, even, if need be, "in paradise." He is being tutored by his secretary, Msgr. Thomas Ryan, of Tipperary, Ireland. This has caused many whimsical comments about the Pope's Irish brogue, but he really speaks English with an Italian accent.

A news photo during President Eisenhower's Vatican visit in December, 1959, showed the Pope and the President laughing heartily. Newspapers received calls from readers who wished to be in on the joke. It was explained that when Pope John was about to read a six-hundred-word speech in English he turned to Eisenhower and remarked, *"Ora ne senti una bella."* The President's interpreter, Col. Vernon Walter, had made the translation: "This is going to be a beaut!"

John has not tried to follow Pius XII's practice of carefully preparing a special message for each professional or trade group arriving at the Vatican. Pius wanted to give advice that would be pertinent to the occupation of those in the audience. John, however, thinks that people need to hear the simple religious truths reiterated.

Three thousand persons who gathered at Castel Gandolfo one summer's day heard him say, "I know we all feel a tendency to tell lies in order to avoid any sort of trouble, but you must remember that truth, charity, and love are three of the most important principles of the Church."

In his first few months he made twenty-five trips outside

Vatican walls. Friendly punsters in Rome tabbed him "Johnny Walker." One winter's day no one could find him. The word went out: "The Pope is missing!" There were wild, wonderful scenes of dismay. Finally, after an hour and a half, he was found visiting a home for old priests some miles from the Vatican.

Another time he was discovered at the Pontifical Roman Seminary with the rector, Msgr. Pio Paschini, an old friend, telling the seminarians stories of his own youth. He also told them about a retreat master who gave a talk on purgatory. The priest became carried away with this subject; he began yelling, "Fire! Fire!" with such vigor that people who lived near the school came rushing into the street to see the blaze.

The Italian Government, which felt responsible for the Pope's safety in Rome, finally stationed two motorcycle policemen at the exit of the papal palace. They would move into position whenever John's car came out, whether he wanted them to or not.

A few days after his election Pope John expressed a desire to travel to the famous shrine in Lourdes. Again the officials of the Vatican were thrown into consternation. In modern times a papal trip of the kind was unprecedented, and, it was argued, there were solid reasons why it should remain unprecedented. If the Pope were going to travel to shrines in far-off places, Catholics all over the world would expect a papal visit.

Apparently John was convinced by the argument. In one large audience he said he never expected to travel far from the Vatican. "I am happy that so many of you come here," he said, "since the duties of the pontificate force me to sacrifice ever seeing my native town again, or of traveling afar except when my benediction will no longer be needed." He was indicating that his death would be the next long journey he would take.

On the ninth of each month Pope John goes to a tomb in St. Peter's basilica lettered simply "Pius P.P. XII." He kneels and meditates. Once he even had his motorcycle escort join him at the tomb.

On one of the walls of his study he has hung paintings of the five Popes he has known in his lifetime: Leo XIII, St. Pius X, Benedict XV, Pius XI, and Pius XII. He has said that each of them contributed to the honor he now receives. Those five men made the Church young and resilient and aware in worldly matters.

They also made the Church as strong spiritually as it has ever been in all its history. Now it is Pope John's turn.

Laughter in Our Family

୫

BY PHYLLIS McGINLEY

Happy families are alike in many ways. For one thing, they own a surface similarity of good cheer. Also, they like each other, which is quite a different thing from loving. And they usually have a purseful of domestic humor accumulated against rainy days. This humor is not necessarily witty. The jokes may be incomprehensible to outsiders, and the laughter spring from utterly trivial sources. But the jokes and the laughter are valuable because they belong to the families.

Our own family is probably no gayer than any other group of four persons who enjoy each other's company. Still, we have all lived together a long time and our purse is well supplied. We are forever reaching into it for an anecdote.

"Do you remember the picnic when a horse ate our lunch? Do you remember how Daddy always dressed up in a white coat and tied a towel around his head when he took our temperatures? Do you remember the treasure hunt when everybody forgot where we'd hidden the treasure?" We are always asking ourselves questions of that kind.

"Khrushchev" is not a funny name, but we never hear it without smiling because that is what Patsy used to call her handkerchief when she was four. No one ever remarks that a friend's phone is tied up without our harking back to little Julie's first witticism.

On her toy telephone she intently dialed a number. "Hello," she said, "is this the zoo? I want to speak to the lion."

There was a suitable silence. Then, turning to me, she said solemnly, "The lion is busy."

We carefully preserve an Easter card which Patsy painted for us when she was six. There had been a bad drought that spring and she had heard much about conserving water. The card was a masterpiece of mingled pagan and religious art, with rabbits competing for importance with crosses and lilies. She gave it to us folded over like a book. Inside she had drawn three balloons, each with its appropriate legend. The first exclaimed, "Happy Easter!" The second announced that "Christ is Risen!" The third said simply, "Save Water."

When the girls were small we were wary about quoting their sayings. Children do not like to be laughed at. Now, though, they listen greedily when we remind them of unconscious *bon mots* from their youth.

And, after all, it is not everyone who can so well sum up the difficulties of virtuous behavior as did our youngest one night at table. We had been discussing, of all things (and we have always discussed all things), saints. We were claiming favorites among them.

"Which saint would you like best to be?" we asked her.

"Oh," she said firmly, "I'd choose to be a martyr."

We gaped, unbelieving. But she had her reasons marshaled. "You see, you only have to be a martyr once," she said.

Some of our favorite stories have a pathetic overtone, like clown's comedy. I dare not name which daughter it was who, in second grade, found $1 in a vacant lot on the way home from school. Honest creature that she was, she went up and down the block for an hour, knocking at each door to inquire if anyone had lost a fortune. We live in a scrupulous village, so no one claimed it. She brought the dollar proudly home to tuck into her bank. After having reassured her that finders of such anonymous wealth were certainly keepers, I asked, "Did you ever find any money before?"

"Oh, yes," she told me. "Once I found a dime under a tree. But I put it back."

No wonder I still worry about the child, even now that she is grown up!

The whole family laughs at me, but not at my jokes, which are rare. What they recall most hilariously are the scrapes I get into through my total lack of mechanical ability. They long ago stopped commenting on the fact that I can't cope with a pencil sharpener or efficiently defrost a refrigerator.

They no longer expect me to read a road map or assemble a food chopper. But when I once got locked for hours into my shower stall by pulling the shower door straight through the jamb instead of pushing it properly out—a feat of idiot strength unparalleled by Atlas—it made them happy as crickets.

It is my husband's wit, though, that we chiefly savor.

"Here comes Daddy," Julie sang out once when she was a very small girl, waiting at the window for him. "He brings fun! He brings joy! He brings the paper."

The compliment with a sting in its tail is our copyrighted brand of family humor. But she was a wise child. She knew her own parent and realized early that a cheerful father is as important as he is rare. My husband's jests will not make a Hollywood fortune. Bennett Cerf will never collect his pearls for a column. *We* collect them, though, and tell our beads with mirth.

I have said that he is a wit and I stand by that. He is not, however, a raconteur. He has no patience with a manufactured joke. He is as likely to betray the point of one by telling it backward as he is to coin a personal epigram. At those, in our minds, he excels.

"Children should be herded but not seen," he instructed our first nursemaid, quite untruthfully. And he asked me once plaintively why our kids must "always run downstairs at the tops of their voices?"

"I have a phenomenal memory," he told a friend of ours who boasted of his steel-trap mind. "I can forget anything."

We do not disdain puns in our limited circle and we still delight in the social criticism he let fly one evening. The occasion was a theater benefit for a Worthwhile Charity. But charity turned out to be very dressy, indeed; the orchestra was full of white ties and evening gowns. "Don't you think" he asked me between acts, "that this is rather putting on the underdog?"

I have always cherished his comment on an exceedingly broken-down Victorian chair which I brought home from an auction. "Ah," he said appreciatively. "Custom built, no doubt, for the Hunchback of Notre Dame."

Yet it is his unpremeditated witticisms which we most greedily collect. For he is a man impatient with the confines of language. Words get in his way and he meets them head-on. His "dwelf" is ever so much better than "dwarf" or even "elf," we believe, as a description of something gnomish.

"And I fell for it," I heard him murmur after one of our girls had brought off a teasing coup. "Fell for it—pipeline and sinker."

"I'm so tired I can't keep open," may have a peculiar sound, but how completely fitting it is to describe a state of enervation! We repeat it after him with relish. And we like the way he described a recent acquisition of the household. Dido, our savage but beautiful black cat, was suddenly a mother. My husband rejoiced. (He likes cats.) He came up from a look at the new nursery, beaming and too enthusiastic to rummage through his vocabulary for the exact word. What he invented was far more expressive. "There she is, proud as Lucifer," he told us, "with that batter of kittens swirming around her." Certainly *batter* is a splendid term for kittens and *swirming*, which must be a combination of "squirming" and "swarming," has elements of genius.

We also cherish Dad's description of a certain gossip as "living from mouth to mouth" and of a critic we know as "earning his bread in the sweat of his highbrow." And we never take an auto trip together that we do not keep in mind his deathless admonition, "We're in a hurry. We haven't time to take a short cut."

If it is true, as he once misquoted Thoreau, that "the mass of men lived lives of quiet exasperation," then such recollections as these are the balm.

I have been dipping into our private purse at random. The supply is nearly limitless but many of the happenings which in memory cause us the most mirth would not stir anyone but us. These are private treats, privately arrived at. Half of them depend on the joy of recognition. Some of them are as esoteric as runes.

Which reminds me of the first time *esoteric* became a family joke. I must explain that, at postkindergarten age, Pat liked to consider herself never an outsider on anything. "Yes, I know" was a phrase often on her tongue, whether we were discussing modern art, gardening, or child psychology. She was also old enough to be interested in words but young enough to take them literally.

"Your father makes esoteric jokes," I once remarked at dinner.

"What does *that* mean?" she demanded promptly.

"Esoteric?" I said, always happy to inform the young idea.

"Oh, that refers to something private or hidden, something which is known to only a few people."

"Yes, I know," she said automatically.

There was a brief pause and then came her station announcement. "Yes, I *do* know. And I know the people, too."

After all, it's knowing the people that gives a jest its flavor.

Women Are Funny

ح

BY JOHN E. GIBSON

Women are funny in lots of ways. They are capricious, contrary, inconsistent—full of enigmatic complexities. The average man stopped trying to figure them out long ago.

But science did not. In universities and research institutions psychologists and sociologists have been exploring the foibles of the fair sex, coming up now and then for air or to exclaim over feminine idiosyncrasies. Let us take a look at some of their most interesting findings.

Are women more superstitious than men?

Yes. When it comes to walking under ladders or avoiding black cats, women are the most superstitious human beings ever invented. A Gallup Poll has shown that women regard breaking a mirror on Friday the thirteenth with far more apprehension than men do. A great many women do not like to see a pair of shoes left standing unless the right shoe is on the right side. Others would not dream of cutting their fingernails on Friday.

The throw-spilled-salt-over-your-shoulder school also includes a large faction who, when getting dressed, always put on their shoes and stockings first. Then there are those whose idiosyncrasies concern numbers, like the farm wife who, when canning fruit, always makes sure there are an even number of pieces in the jars before screwing on the lid.

Scientists have a number of theories about why women are more superstitious than men. Some believe it is closely tied in with their "intuitive promptings."

Are most women good judges of how attractive they are?

No! Studies show that most women regard themselves as far better-looking than they actually are. Tests conducted on women students at Brooklyn College, New York City, showed that the less good-looking a girl is, the more she is likely to overestimate her attractiveness. Best judges of their own looks were the girls rated most attractive by others.

Conclusion of the investigators: unless a girl is really pretty, what she sees in the mirror is colored by wishful thinking.

Is it true that though women spend millions of dollars a year on perfume, most cannot tell one scent from another?

Yes. Not only that, but tests show that they often have trouble telling the difference between cheap perfumes and expensive ones. Research scientists Bernard Locke and Charles H. Grimm studied a cross section of college women, ranging from nineteen to fifty, who had been using perfume from one to twenty-five years.

Most couldn't tell expensive perfumes from cheap ones. Many rated expensive perfumes as inexpensive, and vice versa. Another study showed that most women could not tell the difference between perfumes ranging in cost from 50¢ to $16 an ounce.

When asked to identify such common scents as rose, lilac,

gardenia, and jasmine, the ladies scored correctly only 23 percent of the time. And only one in four could correctly identify
the rose, popular as it is.

Is it true that women are harder to please than men?

Few questions have been more strongly debated. Men assert
that women are contrary creatures whose whims are impossible
to predict and whose desires are impossible to satisfy. And
women retort that no matter how hard you try, you simply
can't please a man.

Psychologists at Wayne University, Detroit, made a careful
survey of men and women students. They gave each group a
series of personality tests. The women tended to respond un-
pleasantly to a far wider variety of situations than did the men.
They were also much more easily annoyed by trifles and much
quicker to show their annoyance when things were not "just
so." Men submitted uncomplainingly to inconveniences that
made the ladies blow their tops.

Studies at the University of Cincinnati have shown that
women are much harder to please than men are. Women were
found to have far more food dislikes than men and to be much
more critical of how each dish was prepared.

What are women most afraid of? ·

Perhaps the most scientific attempt to provide an answer to
this question has been made by psychologists at Alabama College, Montevallo, where the fears of one thousand college
women were carefully cataloged. The average woman, the investigators found, admitted to a total of seventy-eight fears.
Topping the list were snakes, insane persons, mad dogs, being
accosted by drunken men, firearms, burglars, and hornets or
spiders.

Contrary to popular notions, the average woman was *not*

found to be particularly afraid of mice. Most women could take their mice in stride, but many admitted fear of the larger un-domesticated animals. Most had no fear of becoming old maids, but many were afraid of being disappointed in love.

The study showed that the number of fears each woman had was directly related to her intelligence: the higher her IQ, the fewer the things she feared.

Is there any truth in the average housewife's complaint that by the time she is finished with cooking, cleaning, taking care of the children, and all the rest of the household chores, she has little or no time left for leisure?

It is true if she does not count the time she spends reading, chatting over the back fence, attending club meetings, listening to the radio, watching television, or engaging in other recreation.

Social researchers at Purdue University, Lafayette, Indiana, decided to settle the following questions scientifically. Does the average housewife have any leisure time? And if so, how much? They sent scores of investigators to observe the housewife in her natural habitat. Altogether, 1,260 families were surveyed.

Most housewives had between two and three hours of leisure every day. Some had as much as five hours. Rural housewives did not have quite as soft a touch as city ones, but the average urban housewife with three children had three hours of leisure. Those with fewer children had even more time on their hands and those with larger families correspondingly less. Women with five children averaged about one hour.

This study did not go into the matter of how much household drudgery the average wife had succeeded in foisting on her husband. Once when a husband came home from a rough day at the office, nothing stood between him and his pipe and slippers. Apparently this is no longer the case, for a nationwide survey by the American Institute of Public Opinion shows that six out of ten husbands help with the housework, 40 percent lend a hand with the cooking, and nearly a third wash dishes at home either "all the time" or "frequently." Science's findings suggest that maybe it's the man's work that's never done.

Two-Car Family

໕ঌ

BY JOHN J. RYAN

Walking home from the railroad station, a mere two miles, I fondly recall those days five years ago when we were a one-car family. My wife did not know how to drive. My eldest son was twelve and his only interest in anything on wheels was his hope of getting a new bike for Christmas.

I was then a little chubby. I drove to and from the station, morning and evening. I would ride around the corner to get a pack of cigarettes. My family was lean and hard from walking to the stores, school, and just about every place else. It never occurred to them to ride.

Car costs were modest: low insurance, and $3 of gas and oil now and then, never more often than every two weeks. Tires lasted forever, it seemed; they got little wear. One week I put on only fourteen miles.

Then one fateful Saturday morning I noticed I was the only man in the supermarket. The women would take their sackfuls to their cars and drive home. Their husbands were probably still in bed, I figured. If I could get my wife to drive it would mean a life of ease for me. So I taught her to drive.

Things immediately went to the worms.

My family gave up walking. My wife drove the kids to school; drove son Kevin on his newspaper route each day; drove to the supermarket twice a day. She joined the Bowling League, the PTA, and nearly every other organization within fifty miles.

The family was getting soft and fat. I was getting lean and hard. Once in a while, late at night, I would get a chance to drive the car by myself, generally to put it into the garage.

The only thing my wife put into the car was the key. I filled it with gas; changed the oil; checked the air in the tires, water in the battery, and antifreeze in the radiator; and, of course, I washed and waxed it. She, in turn, would sometimes manage to put 375 miles on it in one week without going more than ten blocks from home.

At last, reluctantly, I decided that perhaps we needed a second car.

"Keen, Dad," said my twelve-year-old who wasn't twelve anymore. He was now seventeen and taking a course in driver education at school. "I'll help pay for it," he said. "I'll get a part-time job."

He did, too. I paid $1,000 for a used car and he chipped in $22.50.

For this he became a partner. But not for long. The day he got his license I seemed to get frozen out of the partnership. He began referring to "his" car. Now we had two cars and three drivers and I found I was walking more than ever.

And the costs! The insurance alone for two cars and three drivers, one of whom is a boy under twenty-five, is staggering. The two cars use so much gas I am surprised the gasoline company doesn't suggest filling them directly from the tank truck. And with ten tires to rotate, put air into, and replace!

I have a fourteen-and-a-half-year-old son who counts the minutes until he, too, is seventeen and can drive a car. He is full of promises of chipping in to buy it, driving me places, and picking me up at the station, but I know what will happen. We will have three cars, four drivers, and I'll still be walking.

Well, not quite. I was just down in the basement looking at the five-year-old English racer. If I raise the seat, fix the chain, and take off those foxtails . . .

Computer Cussedness

BY ROBERT C. LUNCH

Millions of bills and receipts are being printed and mailed at this moment by thousands of computers. Among them will be at least several thousand mistakes which will cause tears, laughter, or ulcers.

Consider the case of the grandmother who bought her grandson a crib. She charged it and had it sent to grandson's address. When grandson was six months old, father received a bill for $83.50 from the store.

"Well," he thought, "a simple error, easily fixed."

Father wrote to the store explaining that this bill should be sent to grandmother. Next month he received another bill. He wrote again. After six months and six bills from the store, wife called grandmother.

"But I've already paid for it!" said grandmother.

After a year, during which father had replied to twelve bills, he received a demand from a collection agency to pay up. Father was no longer amused. He sent an angry letter by registered mail to the president of the store, threatening to sue for harassment, loss to his reputation and credit standing, and some mental anguish.

Three days later the mailman delivered a letter of apology. It seems the clerk, in making out the original sales slip, had put an X in the wrong box. The machine that made out the bills could not read father's letters; it read only machine language: holes in IBM cards. The letters had never been read by anyone.

This is not unusual. In many cases machine-made bills bear a printed warning that letters are not to be sent in with payment checks, but rather in a separate envelope, usually to another address. Because of machine inability to read ordinary language, such mistakes are becoming increasingly common. The machine cannot read; it simply continues, haughtily, to grind out its past errors.

On October 22, 1965, the UPI reported from Fresno, California, that a professor had ordered three books from a book club, only to have the wrong ones arrive. The right books did not arrive until months later, too late to be of use. But the computer kept grinding out bills for the returned books. One day brought four bills.

The professor wrote to the computer, starting his letter, "Dear Computer": and ending, "I don't owe you any money; honest, I don't."

The letter fell into the hands of the company treasurer. He wrote the usual letter of apology and offered to send three books free. "I promise to send them secretly so that our computers won't be aware of it," he wrote. "We are attempting to calm the machine and make it forget you."

Although the percentage of errors is very low, almost every family has had at least one experience in trying to get a machine statement corrected. Why is it so difficult? The reasons are various, but the most important is the almost religious belief that a computer cannot make a mistake.

Computers can and do make mistakes. All that need happen is

for a random pulse to double in amplitude for a millionth of a second or for a pulse to be delayed in the circuit for the same length of time. If it adds an extra "one" in the wrong column you could get a bill or check for $1,000 or $1,000,000 instead of $1, or vice versa. The employee who earns $100 a week and gets a check for $1,000,000 usually winds up on the front page. The mistakes that really hurt are seldom publicized. Some of the funny ones aren't publicized either.

The computer is an idiot. It can do only three things: add one at a time, subtract one at a time, or do nothing. From a purely technical viewpoint the last is just as important as the first two.

Consider the case of Joe Sacramento, who needed a new TV set in time for the football season and it was another week until payday. Fortunately Joe had an A-1 credit rating. He could put down $10, promise to pay $10 a month for another twenty-four months, and take home a set. A week later he got his pay, so he sent the store a check for the full amount.

Six months later he received a bill from a finance company. He called the store; they promised to straighten it out. Next month he received another bill from the same finance company. Again he called the store. Six months later he was still receiving a bill each month and calling the store each month.

One evening he came home and found his wife in hysterics. "The finance company called," she sobbed. "If we don't pay up right away, they're going to sue."

The next morning Joe called his attorney and found it would cost him $500 to bring the case to court. In desperation he called the district attorney to see if he could lodge a criminal complaint. He couldn't. He called the Better Business Bureau. "No," they said, "we can't enter into legal disputes." But they did give him the name and unlisted phone number of the store manager.

"I called you," Joe told him, bending the truth, "to inform you that I am suing for harassment and wanted to make certain we got your name spelled correctly on the subpoena."

The store manager was shocked. "I'll correct the mistake," he said, "if I personally have to go to Arizona and tear our central computer apart." Two days later a letter of apology and a receipt for full payment arrived by messenger. The letter assured Joe that the mistake had been corrected and that he would not hear from the finance company again.

Weeks later it was discovered that the store had paid off Joe's account with the finance company. But the hole in the card had been punched imperfectly, leaving a small fragment of paper where the hole should have been. The machine, not sensing a hole which indicated payment, had done nothing about entering the payment, and had proceeded to grind out bills, notices, demands for payment, and, finally, an order to a clerk to telephone the delinquent customer.

A customer once bought a garden implement through the catalogue department of a chain store. When the tool proved to be defective he returned it to the local store of the chain. A few weeks later he was notified that the store had credited $230 to his account. Since he was an honest man he wrote back to explain that he had not paid for the implement and that the store did not owe him anything.

A few days later the store replied to his letter. They insisted they had no record of the transaction; would he please tell them what sort of item he claimed to have purchased and then returned? Before the tale ended, more than fifty documents and explanations had been sent back and forth. When the matter was finally settled, the customer had an inch-thick file of correspondence.

In a surprising number of instances everyone will admit the computer has gone awry, yet nothing can be done to correct the mistake. One bank in California flatly refused to refund $2 incorrectly charged to a depositor. It would, they explained, cost hundreds of dollars to correct the error, so they offered, instead, to take him and his wife out for a night on the town and charge it to public relations!

Computers are very expensive and can be justified only if they can be used continually. Stopping them to correct mistakes is costly. Some are programmed to stop at an exact time each day for corrections. If, however, for any reason, the correction is not made at that time, the mistake remains in the tape and multiplies.

Many companies use a central computer. Correcting a mistake in such cases requires extra steps in coding and mailing. If the central record in a large corporation is wrong, the coded cards needed to correct the mistake multiply like bacteria.

Such central records can be a nuisance even when no mistake is involved. At one large store in California there is no way for the personnel to tell the customer the amount of his current bill. If he decides to pay off his bill in full he must wait for his next machine-made statement.

No store manager, banker, or finance company will say so publicly, but privately they will admit that the growing volume of mistakes has them worried. "They drive us nuts," said a public-relations man, off the record. "They give our store a bad name and we know that those who complain like to tell their friends."

During the last session of the California legislature a bill was introduced which would make it a crime not to correct a mistake that hurt a person's credit rating.

The California Consumers' Council has received hundreds of complaints. Even though a computer is incredibly fast, getting out the bills may be no faster than before. By the time the coded information is sent from one city to another, interest is often added to revolving charge accounts that have been paid in full. When the monthly interest-due date arrives, the checks are still waiting to be fed into the computer which, knowing no better, charges the unwarranted interest.

A friend of mine now buys for cash only. A computer skipped a hole in a punched card, so now, though he has never defaulted on a debt, his credit rating at the retail-credit association says he is a bad risk. He has canceled all his credit cards. He even refuses to pay by check.

If enough Americans follow his lead, businessmen will suffer where it hurts most, in falling sales. Meanwhile the tranquilizer business, at least, is booming.

MOM

A woman knocked at a neighbor's door and was surprised when a six-year-old appeared.

"Hello, Sue," she said. "Are you here all alone?"

"Yes," replied the child. "Mom's in the hospital and me and Daddy and Donald and Janet and Bobbie are here all alone."

Clarence Roeser.

THE REASON WHY

"You two certainly get on well," the pastor said to the couple celebrating their silver wedding anniversary. "Don't you ever have any differences of opinion?"

"Yes, we do," the wife answered, "but we never tell each other about them."

Ernest Blevins.

WITHOUT OPTION

Dad, a traveling salesman, was on one of his visits home. He volunteered to take care of the kids one night so Mom could have an evening out. At bedtime he sent the youngsters up to bed and settled down to read. One of the children kept creeping down the stairs, but Dad kept sending him right back.

At 9:30 the doorbell rang. It was Mrs. Cooper, the next-door neighbor, who asked if her son was there.

"No," Dad promptly replied.

Just then a little head appeared over the banister and a voice shouted, "I'm here, Mom, but he won't let me go home!"

A. T. Quigg.

FIRST AMONG HIS PEERS

Discipline in the large family was becoming progressively worse, so the harried mother gathered her brood together and presented a plan.

"I'm going to keep a record of the behavior of each of you," she announced. "On Saturday the member of the family who has been most obedient will get a reward."

"That's not fair!" exclaimed one of the youngsters. "Daddy will win it every time!"

F. G. Kernan.

EVER GREEN

In a supermarket in Detroit a sign read: "Lettuce will not turn brown if you put your head in a plastic bag before placing it in the refrigerator."

Clarence Roeser.

WHAT A GRANDMOTHER IS

A grandmother is a lady who has no children of her own, so she likes other people's little girls. A grandfather is a man grandmother. He goes for walks with the boys and they talk about fishing and tractors and like that.

Grandmas don't have to do anything except be there. They're old, so they shouldn't play hard or run. It is enough if they drive us to the market where the pretend horse is and have lots of dimes ready. Or if they take us for walks, they should slow down past things like pretty leaves or caterpillars. They should never, ever say "Hurry up."

Usually they are fat, but not too fat to tie kids' shoes. They wear glasses and funny underwear. They can take their teeth and gums off.

It is better if they don't typewrite, or play cards except with us. They don't have to be smart, only answer questions like why dogs hate cats and how come God isn't married. They don't talk baby talk like visitors do, because it is hard to understand. When they read to us they don't skip, or mind if it is the same story again.

Everybody should try to have one, especially if you don't have television, because grandmas are the only grown-ups who have got time.

Patsey Gray.

NOT NEWS

One Saturday morning my brother had gone to pick up little Dennis at catechism class.

Dennis came skipping down the church steps. "Daddy," he said proudly, "I learned something new today!"

"You did?" said his father. "Tell me what it was."

At that the boy began to recite the Hail Mary. After the first slow careful phrases, his father joined in.

Suddenly Dennis stopped dead in his tracks and looked up at his father. "Aw!" he said, "somebody told you!"

E. Carl.

6 − 1 = 0

My father, a farmer, was undemonstrative. We children used to worry because he never seemed to show our mother proper appreciation for her sweet disposition and the many ways she helped out with the farm work. One afternoon Mother was delayed at a neighbor's house helping with a very sick girl and so did not get home ahead of Father.

Father arrived from the field at the usual time and walked into the big front room where we six children were playing. He stood in the doorway surveying the scene for a moment, then frowned and said, "Where is everybody?"

Then we stopped worrying that mother was not appreciated.

Ernest Blevins.

IN OUR HOUSE

My six-year-old daughter Helen shows the same aversion to good food that so many other children display at dinnertime. One day I found myself spluttering, "Child, you don't care for meat, vegetables, salad, or milk—what *do* you like?"

She regarded me steadily through her big brown eyes. "Why, I like *you*, Daddy!" she replied demurely.

Benjamin Talsky.

GRACE NOTES

The young girl who lives next door was planning a festive birthday. Her fiance was coming for dinner and they were also celebrating their engagement.

Just before lunch a florist's truck drove up in front of her home and a delivery man stepped out with a beautiful bouquet of roses. But the card accompanying the flowers was addressed to her mother. Thinking there must be some mistake, she opened the card and read the message: "I'm so glad it was a girl. Bill."

Ernest Blevins.

PLAYED BY EAR

"Dear," said mother trying to soothe her little Alice, "I thought you said your earache was better. Why do you keep on crying?"

"I'm waiting for Daddy to come home," the youngster replied. "He's never seen me with an earache."

John Novak.

USES OF DIVERSITY

The mother of a large family explained to me why she always dresses her children alike, right down to the youngest baby. "When we had only four children," she told me, "I dressed them alike so that I would be sure of not losing any. But now," she added, glancing proudly at her brood of nine, "I dress them alike so that I can be sure I don't pick up any that don't belong to us."

Paul Houck.

LIGHTS AND SHADOWS

I had just stepped down to the basement to put a load of washing into the machine. As I came back into the kitchen, I heard our six-year-old Bobby just going out the front door, leaving for school. "Oh, are you leaving now?" I called. "Yes, Mommy," he replied, "I left a kiss for you in the refrigerator!"

Mrs. Lawrence Gilbert.

THE BLACKBOARD JUNGLE

A certain gentleman called his sister on the phone one day and was a bit taken aback to have the call answered by his six-year-old nephew, who should at that hour have been in school.

"Why, Danny!" exclaimed the fond uncle. "What are you doing home? Are you all right?"

"Oh, I'm fine!" answered the boy. "I'm sick."

American Weekly.

QUICK CHILL

One bitter cold evening after church Debbie was impatiently waiting for her father to get the car door unlocked. After she declared she was "freezing to death," her father answered, "Oh, I don't think you'll freeze for a few minutes."

"I don't know about that, Daddy," she replied, "I'm already shivering as fast as I can."

Frances Benson.

A CHILD'S UNIVERSE

One day I was peeling onions at the sink and my three-year-old Danny was perched on one of the high stools next to me. By and by I noticed that tears were starting in his eyes.

"Mother, look!" he said. "I just got a drink in my eye!"

CREDIT CARDS

In the old days men rode chargers. Now they marry them.

Harold E. Youngs.

THE BRIGHT SIDE

An anxious father had been pacing throughout the night in a little waiting room just outside the maternity ward of a hospital. At long last his wife's doctor appeared.

"Everything went just fine," he said reassuringly. "I know you wanted a boy, but I'm sure you will be just as happy when you see your beautiful new daughter."

The new father flashed a weak smile and replied, "Oh, sure, Doctor! That's perfectly OK by me. As a matter of fact, a girl was my second choice."

Modern Medicine.

PAY DAY

People call it take-home pay because there is no other place you can afford to go with it.

Philadelphia Evening Bulletin.

"Dad, in English class they keep talking about a 'Grecian urn.' What's a Grecian urn?" a teen-ager inquired.

"I don't know," replied the father. "I suppose it depends on what he does for a living."

J. J. Kelly.

THE LIMIT

Six-year-old Chuck went fishing with his grandfather and proudly returned home with two fish. "This one's a perch," he explained excitedly to his mother, "and this one's a loudmouth bass!"

Wall Street Journal.

TRIAL BY WIRE

I

She dialed Information to get a phone number. She had pencil and paper ready.

"The number," said the operator, "is Capital five—five, five, five, five."

After a short silence the caller asked, "How do you make a capital five?"

Apostolate of Our Lady.

II

I was very pleasantly surprised to see my teen-aged daughter answer the phone and then hang up in fifteen minutes instead of her usual hour. I congratulated her on having kept her conversation so brief and then asked her which of her friends she had been talking to.

"Oh," she explained, "that wasn't a friend. It was a wrong number."

Roberta Rich.

TO SEE STEADILY, TO SEE WHOLE

A mother whose six-year-old son attends a Milwaukee public school tells this story about her boy.

"He comes home from his first-grade class every day, very enthusiastic about his teacher. One day I overheard him describing her to his brothers and sisters.

"He said that she is as tall as I am, and just about as big. She is about my age, wears makeup like me, and she scolds the children when they are naughty and reads to them and plays games with them when they are good, just like me.

"I found myself getting anxious to meet this other me. I finally met her when I went to school to see how my son was getting along. When I saw her I hesitated for a minute before asking, in what I am afraid was a rather surprised voice, if she was his teacher.

"In that moment I felt great pride in my son because I realized he had a greater gift than most grown-ups ever acquire in a lifetime: the gift of seeing people for what they really are inside, and not going by their looks. Because, you see, it had never entered his mind to mention the fact that she was colored."

Doyle K. Getter in the Milwaukee Journal.

FLIGHTS OF FANCY

He bore his sorrows like a man: he blamed them on his wife—*Mary C. Dorsey.*

For better or for worse, but not for good.—Farm Journal.

He could say No like a man driving a rivet—*William B. Mowers.*

Women chatter boxing—*Patricia Orrok.*

The haves, the have-nots, and the charge-its.—*Earl Wilson.*

The loudest sound known to man is the first rattle in a brand new car.—*Earl Wilson.*

Always putting his foot down when he didn't have a leg to stand on.—*E. Carlson.*

Kept her children so clean I thought they were for sale.—*Phyllis Diller.*

X THIS HEALTHY LIFE

Illustration from *Diary of a Quitter*

Diary of a Quitter

ॐ

BY RALPH REPPERT

Sunday. Too much party last night and so a cigarette hangover today. Even my blood hurts. I think I will break the smoking habit.

Monday. Come on, will power! I keep saying to myself, "I don't *want* a cigarette!" And deep within me a small voice keeps answering, "The heck you don't!"

Tuesday. This is supposed to be my edgy day, but I'm fine. Sharp. Alert. I never noticed before how much noise our cat makes stomping around the house.

I guess I won't have a highball. Alcohol makes you want to smoke. My wife Harriet suggests a warm bath to soothe my nerves.

Wednesday. My neighbor George Peeble quits smoking every month or so. He says to eat fruit and lay off starches and fats, because kicking the cigarette habit makes a man put on weight.

Breakfast today: sliced apple, quartered orange, eight grapes, raw carrot. And another warm bath.

Thursday. I knew my sliced apple, quartered orange, eight grapes, and raw carrot for breakfast reminded me of something. It's what they give the monkeys at the zoo.

Most people who quit smoking get irritable on the fourth day, but not me. My abstinence has nothing to do with the things I said today. I've *always* hated broccoli and dog acts on TV.

Another warm bath. I lay in the tub and noticed how badly the bathroom needs painting.

I have given up TV. It makes me thirsty for a highball and highballs make me want to smoke.

Friday. I can honestly say that quitting cigarettes is as easy as taking candy from a baby. (Did you ever try taking candy from a baby?)

My sense of smell, which flew the coop when I began smoking years ago, has come home to roost. Today I took Aunt Garnet to the station, put her on the train for Wilkes-Barre, and kissed her good-bye. Aunt Garnet smokes. It was like kissing Rocky Colavito.

My taste buds, deadened by years of smoking, have begun to flex their little muscles again. I can taste toothpaste. I can't stand it.

Saturday. Two warm baths today. My fingers are wrinkled like prunes.

Another monkey breakfast. I have forgotten how to use a fork.

I have given up running errands for my wife. Running errands makes me want to watch TV, which makes me want a highball, which makes me want to smoke.

If there is one thing I am *not*, it's a man like my uncle Louis. When he quit drinking he went around knocking highballs out of people's hands. I see other people smoking. I don't try to influence them. I don't try to scare them. I don't pity them. I *envy* them.

226

Sunday. I cannot look another apple, orange, grape, or raw carrot in the face. Coffee for breakfast.

Another warm bath. Discovered something interesting: warm baths make me want to smoke. So do cold baths. So does going without a bath.

I've saved some money. No cigarettes for a week—two packs a day at 30¢ a pack—that's $4.20.

Backed out of the garage and, in a nervous twitch that never happened before, broke a taillight. The man at the filling station has ordered me a new one. For $4.20.

After a week without smoking I feel I am the captain of my soul, the master of my fate. While feeling so masterful, have decided I *want* to smoke.

Took a warm bath. Mixed a stiff highball. Lit a cigarette. I am the cleanest coward in Baltimore.

The Heart and Mind
of Pope John

৪৯

BY HENRI DANIEL-ROPS

The reign of John XXIII was barely five years long. No pontificate in a hundred years had been so short. But none was more significant. The future of Christianity would not have been the same without this large, smiling man.

In 1958 the press interpreted Pope John's election as a pause for the Church. Yet, as the theologian Karl Rahner remarked, "The transitional Pope gave the Church transition toward the future."

The new Pontiff did not take spectacular steps or revoke what those before him had done. He did not change, for instance, the coronation ceremony, which many find inadequate for our times.

Quietly, gently, protocol was simplified. Veneration addressed not to the dignity of the Vicar of Christ but to the person of the man was discreetly dropped. Thus the cheers which had resounded through St. Peter's when the Pope was carried in were stopped by having the people sing.

Pope John took walks in the country which, farmer that he was, he said he could not miss. But he also walked often in the streets of Rome. You could find him in the jails visiting prisoners, even those whom officials had not wanted him to meet. You could see him leaving the Vatican to go to Assisi and to Loreto. Until he died rumors persisted that he was planning to visit Lourdes.

These small acts were significant. They tended to shatter the glass wall behind which Popes seemed to live, isolated from the human community, inaccessible amid the imposing salons of the Vatican Palace. The changes tended to bring Pope John (who, after all, was the successor of a fisherman) closer to those he guided. It was this intention that the people of Rome and the world recognized.

His visits to the Roman suburbs showed how close "Good Pope John" was to his people. On Sunday this eighty-year-old man would exert himself to travel to residential parishes far from the city's center in order to prove that he had not forgotten he was Bishop of Rome.

All along his route the crowds would gather, seven or eight deep. They waited two or three hours even on bitter days. Long before his car came in sight, a great shouting could be heard, an explosion of hurrahs, applause, with horns blowing.

When Pope John arrived, dressed in red cape, sitting high in his car, the cheers doubled. From every window heads peered over draped spreads embroidered especially for the occasion. At some crossroads the Pope made a brief, impromptu speech, something between a lesson from the catechism and a family chat, which was a special grace of his. Sometimes a witty remark made the crowd laugh. He left smiling and giving blessings amid a chorus of thanks.

It had been years since Romans saw such a sight. Less than a century ago Pope Pius IX's funeral had to be held at night to avoid riots. John's popularity was a kind of living witness to the success of his mission.

All this was astonishing, this and what followed. Because, in fact, Angelo Roncalli was quite misunderstood. Some of the fault was his. His manner misled some: they thought him a jolly fat man without too much intelligence. In Paris Papal Nuncio Roncalli's reputation was of one who talked all the time, scarcely listened, and took up his visitors' time with a thousand subjects that had nothing to do with the matter at hand. Besides, he enjoyed his own wit and exercised it with disconcerting frequency.

To believe all this would be to understand very little. For in this flow of words—intentional without doubt—an alert person could catch, from time to time, a short phrase, generally elliptical and allusive, which was the key to the whole profound thought. And the man whom everyone believed to a distracted rambler was perfectly capable of repeating to you six months later a phrase you said to him which he seemed not to be listening to.

In fact, to everyone who knew him well, he revealed himself as quite different from the talkative and laughing prelate. John's was an astonishingly lucid intelligence, capable of penetrating persons and situations. He made his judgments slowly but decisively on the things he considered essential, but his judgments were accompanied by an indulgence for the foolishness and vanity of mortals. The peasant in him showed itself as a king of tranquil realism, of wisdom as old as the world.

Conformist? More inclined certainly to follow tradition than to break with it, he nonetheless tended more than we realize to think for himself, and quite independently. Former French President Vincent Auriol called the Pope "gentle rebel."

But what was as striking about Pope John as his perception

was his generosity. It is not easy to judge men accurately and yet continue to love them. But for him it was natural. He swore that he had nothing to do with it. He said he had since birth been more apt to trust his neighbor and to love him than to mistrust or detest him. And it was in this alliance between his realistic perception and his goodness that the greatness of his pontificate lies.

Goodness was surely the most outstanding quality of his character. It struck his friends long before it was recognized by the general public.

"I want to be kind, always, to everyone." He repeated this hundreds of times. Once, when he was talking about Don Orione, the St. Vincent de Paul of contemporary Italy, he said, "What was admirable about Don Orione is that he always believed that the world could be reconquered by love." Surely Pope John was expressing his own conviction as well.

To reconquer the world for Christ by love. It was his purpose from the moment he became Pope. To do so seemed to him not only in keeping with the Lord's message, but practicable and necessary.

To open the Church to all men of goodwill, to present the most human image of her, the simplest yet the most radiant, to enact Christ's charity in daily life: his decisions, his gestures, reveal this purpose. His realism of mind and generosity of heart united to forge a strategy of goodness, a politics of hospitality.

He thought that only a Church faithful to these ends could stand a chance in the world he saw being born. And everything he did, he did to give the Church a chance.

The Ecumenical Council was Pope John's most important undertaking. From what we can determine, the cardinals gathered in St. Paul Outside the Walls on January 24, 1959, were astounded when the Pope announced the council to them. It had been eighty years and more since the First Vatican

Council had suspended its work. Since then no one dreamed seriously of reopening it. It seemed even that the 1870 dogma of papal infallibility made the decisions of a council relatively useless. Pope John, therefore, broke a spiritual lethargy when he announced his surprising decision.

He said many times that his decision was inspired by the Holy Ghost. But it would not be out of place to relate his decision to his character.

Because John was so humble, he wanted to have the advice of the whole Church in taking positions he thought necessary. Because he was so realistic, he proposed that the council work toward an *aggiornamento*, a bringing-up-to-date of the Church to rid it of the crust of the centuries. Because he was good, he intended to practice the strategy of goodness and he gave the council the stamp of his own character: to be infinitely receptive and generous, in its means as well as in its ends. . . .

What he had to say about the responsibilities of wealth or the absurdity of war made a deep impression. We heard the words of a man talking to mankind. The restraint of these texts shows clearly that "Good Pope John" was capable of being a great statesman. He simply went beyond all politics, toward, we might say, an evangelical politic. . . .

When he died the praise that rose from the whole world was unique for our age. From the Chief Rabbi of Jerusalem to Nikita Khrushchev, men of all creeds joined Catholics in expressing their regrets and their admiration. The Good Pope John, the humble Angelo Roncalli, left a mark in the world so deep that it can never be effaced.

SIGNS

Over a reducing salon: "Thinner Sanctum."

M. B.

ADEPT

Hypochondriac: a person with an infinite capacity for faking pains.

Modern Medicine.

$

After-dinner mint: what you need when the waiter brings the check.

Mrs. Deane Binder.

THE QUIET MEN

A man went to the hospital to visit a friend who was recuperating from a tonsillectomy. As he started up in the elevator the operator asked, "What floor?"

The visitor thought for a moment, then brightened and said crisply, "Men's tonsils, please."

C. Kennedy.

CONFUSION OF TONGUES

In a very, very swank restaurant in Paris an American tourist couple sat fuming. Repeatedly they had tried to catch the waiter's eye, but he ignored them. Finally the husband roared, "Waiter! Can't we get a little service around here?"

"What would you care to have?" the waiter inquired frostily.
"Well, you might begin by bringing us a bottle of your best champagne," replied the American.
"Certainly, monsieur," agreed the waiter. "What year?"
"What do you mean, what year?" demanded the American with rising blood pressure. "Why, *right now!*"

Mrs. Deane Binder.

WHO'S IN CHARGE HERE?

A chap in Stanford, California, looked at the label of a can of "Mixed Nuts" which his wife had purchased. It listed the contents as follows: "Virginia peanuts, cashews, Brazil nuts, almonds, and pecans." He opened the can and counted each and every nut. He found: peanuts 435; cashews 12; Brazil nuts 3; pecans 2; almonds ½.

Saturday Review.

NO END

TV is improving. You used to be able to get a can of beer during a commercial. Now you can go out and rake the lawn.

Fletcher Knebel in the Philadelphia Daily News.

STORMY

A TV weather reporter was so often wrong in his predictions that he became the laughing stock of the community. He applied for a job in another state.
"Why did you leave your previous job?" asked the interviewer.
"The climate didn't agree with me," he replied.

The Far East.

THE DOCTORS' DILEMMAS

A few changes have been made in my waiting room as the result of a recent episode. We had a sign near the doorway: "Have you left anything?" But it had to be removed. A patient stopped before the sign, read it carefully, then turned to my receptionist and remarked, "That sign is wrong! It should read: 'Have you anything left?' "

Modern Medicine.

PSYCHIATRICKS

A woman jumped into a cab and urged the driver to rush her to a downtown building. "I have a two o'clock appointment with my psychiatrist," she said breathlessly. "If I'm not there on time he starts without me."

Clarence Roeser.

FLIGHTS OF FANCY

You can get ulcers before you can get even.—*J. P. McEvoy.*

Executive: a person who follows his work schedule to a tee.— Family Weekly.

The nineteenth hole: where the golfer practices his swig.— *Anna Herbert.*

Compliment: the applause that refreshes.—*F. G. K.*

Hypochondriac: person who can't leave well enough alone. —*Mary C. Dorsey.*

A boiling beach littered with rusty humans.—*Patrick A. Bermingham.*

XI NO CITY OF GOD

Illustration from *I Have This Perfectly Marvelous Woman . . .*

I Heard Jokes Behind the Iron Curtain

ૐ

BY NINO LO BELLO

Behind the Iron Curtain humor is serious. The people know that the pun is mightier than the sword. No matter where you go you hear jokes about the Reds.

I heard this one in each of the Eastern bloc capitals: Sofia, Bucharest, Budapest, Belgrade, East Berlin, Prague, and Warsaw. It seems to be No. 1 on the "Wit Parade."

Three political prisoners are thrown into the same cell but are afraid at first to talk to each other. But at last one blurts out, "I've been in prison since 1953 because I spoke well of Khrushchev." Taking courage, the second says, "And I'm here since 1957 because I spoke evil of Khrushchev." The two men now looked at the third, who reports, "And I'm here because I am Khrushchev."

The Poles seem to defy their regime more openly than the others and the cafes and restaurants in Warsaw are full of loud talk that usually includes the latest joke.

"Piotr" is the little hero of most political anecdotes. Piotr is told by his teacher to write an essay which will be shown to the state school commissar on his inspection tour. Piotr writes: "I have a lovely cat and it has three kittens. All of them are communists." But when the inspector came a few days later, he had changed it: "I have a lovely cat and it has three kittens. Two of them are communists." Asked why he has changed the essay, Piotr replies, "Because one of the kittens opened its eyes this morning."

When Piotr's teacher asks him what makes the communist system superior to others, he responds: "Communism is superior because it adequately copes with difficulties which do not exist in other systems."

Poland's party leader Wladyslaw Gomulka asks little Piotr who his mother is and Piotr says, "The party."

"Excellent!" declares the dictator. "And who is your father, young lad?"

"Gomulka," is the reply.

"Very good!" beams the Red boss. "And what do you want to be when you grow up?"

"An orphan!" says Piotr.

Piotr is quizzed by the teacher: "If one metric ton of coal costs one thousand zlotys and your father orders three thousand zlotys' worth of coal from the state coal agency, how many metric tons will be delivered to your house?" Comes Piotr's answer: "Two and a half metric tons!" When told that this is not correct, Piotr retorts: "I know it's not correct but what can we do? It always happens."

Piotr is older and becomes "Szabo" in Hungary. At a factory meeting Szabo asks the presiding Red official why Hungary, which has so much fertile land, must still import flour; and why, with the high production of textiles, Hungarians go around in shabby clothes. The official says he will have the proper answer next time. At the following meeting, however, another worker rises during the question-and-answer period and says he has only one question: "Where's Szabo?"

Szabo once called dictator Janos Kadar an idiot. For this Szabo is sentenced to fifteen years in prison. Protesting, Szabo points out that the penal code calls for only three months' detention for such an offence.

"We didn't sentence you for offending Comrade Kadar," the judge explains, "but for divulging a state secret."

Szabo tries to get himself arrested and jailed so he will at least have no more financial worries. He goes to an important Communist Party meeting and at an opportune moment shouts, "You Reds are all filthy liars. Kadar is a pig!" He continues yelling insults until the meeting closes. Later the party secretary takes Szabo aside and says, "Man, be careful! What would have happened to you if there had been a real communist present?"

In Bulgaria they tell of an ocean liner that sinks near a tropical island with two men and one woman surviving. If the survivors had been Italian, goes the story, one man would kill the other and live happily ever after with the woman. If the survivors had been French, all three would live together happily ever after. If the survivors had been German, the two men would make war on each other and end up killing themselves and the woman, too. But if the survivors had been Bulgarians, they would wire Moscow for instructions.

In both Bulgaria and Rumania I heard of the two dogs running across their respective borders. As they speed toward each other the Bulgarian dog asks the Rumanian dog why he is leaving Rumania. "So I can get a bone to chew," replies the dog. "And why are you leaving Bulgaria?" "So I can bark," is the answer.

A Bucharest resident goes to the polls and is handed a sealed envelope to drop into the ballot box. He makes the mistake of opening the envelope to examine the names of the candidates, bringing on a loud screech from the election supervisor. "But I wanted to see for whom I was casting my vote," protests the citizen.

"Are you out of your mind?" roars the supervisor. "Don't you know we are a democracy and use the secret ballot?"

I heard the Snow White story in Bucharest when it was brand new, but it went on the grapevine to communist Germany before I got to East Berlin a few days later. Snow White is in her glass coffin. A bird chirps in vain to wake Snow White up and a dwarf gently tickles her now with a feather, without success. Then comes a handsome prince, who whispers something into Snow White's ear. She immediately jumps up. "What was it that you told her?" the prince is asked, and he replies: "I told her that they are selling white thread at the state store."

East Germany's jokes usually have to do with the man who built the infamous Berlin Wall, Boss Walter Ulbricht, easily the most hated of all the communist rulers.

One day, while receiving a medal from Ulbricht, a party member sees a strange telephone on Ulbricht's desk. "Comrade Ulbricht," the hero inquires, "such a funny-looking telephone. It has no mouthpiece, just the receiver. What do you use it for?"

"Well, if you must know," replied Ulbricht, "that is our direct line to Moscow."

On a bright and sunny day Ulbricht walks out of his office with an open umbrella. "But you don't need an umbrella when the sun is shining," declares a comrade.

"I certainly do," replies Ulbricht. "It's raining in Moscow."

Another time, before going off on a vacation, Ulbricht tells one of his stooges to make sure that everything in "the German democratic republic stays in good order during my absence." On his return weeks later a beaming deputy gives his proud report. "During your holiday I have accomplished what the party failed to achieve until now. I opened the wall for a day and we now no longer have a housing shortage. Also, I put your picture on all the altars and at last the churches are empty."

A citizen shows up at the party's central-committee office to ask for Ulbricht. "You can't see him," sayd the office clerk. "Comrade Ulbricht is dead." A half hour later the same man returns and says he wants to talk to Ulbricht.

"I already told you that Comrade Ulbricht is dead." But thirty minutes later the same man is back again. And once again he requests an audience with Ulbricht.

"*Donnerwetter!* I already told you twice that Comrade Ulbricht is dead. How often do you want me to tell you?" Replied the man, "I know, I know. But I can't hear it said often enough."

Ulbricht is more unpopular than Marshal Tito, but the Yugoslavs have their jokes. Tito is the chief of state, the chief of party, and the chief of army. A teacher asks a pupil why Tito holds these three positions. The student answers that nobody in Yugoslavia can live on one job any more.

In Dubrovnik sooner or later you hear, "Tito says that by 1970 we will have an automobile for every five inhabitants, a chicken for every four pots, and a pair of shoes for every three feet."

It was in Belgrade that I heard of the archaeological expedition that brought back a mummy from Egypt. When the Belgrade University scientist could not determine its exact age, they called in the secret police. Four hours later the secret police emerged from the lab and said the mummy was exactly 3,144 years old.

The professors were amazed. They wanted to know how it was done. "Simple," said the secret police. "The mummy confessed."

Letters I Never Sent

ટે>

BY JEAN KERR

Seems to me I used to sleep better before we had all these conveniences. Lately I find that just as I am sinking into that first sweet slumber of the night I suddenly remember I forgot to take a leg of lamb out of the freezer. At this point I have two clear alternatives. I can pad down to the garage and get the lamb, or I can lie there and figure out what else we could have for dinner tomorrow night (either hamburger or what Gilbert, our youngest, calls "creamed chipped beast").

Either way I'm now fully awake, bright-eyed, alert. In fact there seems to be a penetrating sharpness to my mind that I never notice in the daytime. At this moment I feel that I could be profitably reading Toynbee's *A Study of History* or the directions on a Waring blender.

The problem is, of course, to channel this alarming mental energy before I lapse back into that old, disastrous habit of reviewing the low points of my life (the night I swallowed an inlay in the Oak Room at the Plaza; the day I smashed a bottle of mineral oil in the elevator at Saks'; the Sunday that Honey, our cocker spaniel, ate my mother-in-law's wristwatch).

Only recently I discovered that one could put the otherwise lost time to work and make it pay off in terms of mental health, which, I am sure we all agree, becomes more elusive all the time. I just make a list of all the tiny irritations that have been nibbling away at my subconscious and I compose dignified letters of protest. I omit major irritations, like plumbers who make extensive repairs on the wrong bathtub, and dry cleaners who press boys' jackets without removing chocolate bars from pockets. These require stern phone calls.

I find that after I have written one of these letters mentally, I forget the whole matter. The next day my mind is clear to grapple with real problems. And these nocturnal doodlings hurt nobody. I never do type them up in the morning because I'm too sluggish, and on the various occasions when I have suggested that I might really mail one of them, my husband has always stopped me by asking a simple question: "Are you out of your mind?"

I am putting down a few sample letters here, in case another insomniac somewhere would like to be as disagreeable as possible (without repercussions) but hasn't quite got the hang of it.

Acme Novelty Co.
Dear Sirs:

I am writing you about your water guns. They leak. And not out of the muzzle, which would be logical, but out of the top, because the little stopper doesn't fit. And if you put the gun under your pillow (naturally, I don't put it under *my* pillow) the water seeps out and wets the whole mattress.

I really can't imagine why you discontinued the plastic model you featured last year. This was an admirable, indeed an ideal, water gun. It worked perfectly for fifteen minutes and then

245

broke into two equal halves. It was worth 25¢. I wish I could say the same for this year's model.

Distressed Consumer.

The Ever-Krisp Curtain Co.
Dear Sirs:

In what mad burst of whimsy did you adopt the slogan: "These curtains laugh at soap and water"? Now, I begrudge no man his flights of fancy. We are all poets at heart. And when I purchased my Ever-Krisp curtains, I did not really expect them to burst into wild guffaws or even ladylike giggles the first time I put them into the sink. (As a matter of fact, with four small boys and one loud Siamese cat, I don't want to hear *one word* from those curtains.)

But, in my incurable naïveté, I did take your claim to imply that these curtains actually *survived* contact with soap and water. I don't mean I expect them to remain ever-krisp. I'm quite accustomed to ever-limp curtains. I did, however, expect them to remain ever-red with ever-white ruffles. As it happens, they are now a sort of off-pink strawberry ripple, which of course doesn't go with my kitchen at all.

Ever-Disgusted.

The Pilgrim Laundry
Dear Sirs:

For years I've rather admired the crisp little messages that appear on that paper strip that is wrapped around the shirts when they come back from your laundry. The sentiments expressed may not have been very original or very imaginative ("Merry Christmas," "Have a Safe Fourth of July") but one felt there was a nice spirit there, and if the tone was sometimes a shade didactic, it was never carping.

246

Well, gentlemen, you must try to imagine my shock when, last week, I discovered the new message, "Have you kissed your wife this morning?" I don't know what *you* call this, but I call it prying. Furthermore, my husband never sees these wrappers because I tear them off before I pile the shirts in the drawer.

Because I have a sincere interest in consumer research, I decided to show one of these strips to my husband and test his reaction. What he said was this: "You tell that laundry that if I had a wife who ironed my shirts, I'd kiss her."

Now, Pilgrims, THINK! Surely you never meant to stir up that little kettle of fish. Not only does it lead to apartness, or whatever is the opposite of togetherness, but one sees how easily it could boomerang on the whole laundry business. You were just trying to help, I know. But let me suggest that you concentrate on those shirts. Would you sew the buttons back on and try not to press the wrinkles *into* the collars, please?

Thanks.

Bergdorf Goodman
Dear Sirs:

In Sunday's paper you had an advertisement for "a casual little go-everywhere frock at $125." Now, what I want to know is, just exactly how casual is this dress? I mean, it isn't *too* casual, is it? Would it really give one a feeling of social security and a sense of "belonging" in the A & P? If you wore it to Parents Night and had to talk to the principal, would it perhaps seem just a trifle slapdash?

Bergdorf's, oh Bergdorf's, can you hear me? You must come down off that mountaintop. I'm afraid you've been overprotected. People you trusted have been keeping things from you.

Promise you won't get mad if I tell you something: you're on the wrong track. I know women who spend that kind of money on clothes. (Well, I don't exactly know them. I overhear them

247

talking during the intermissions at first nights.) But I feel myself to be on solid ground when I say that, at $125, they're not looking for a frock, they're looking for a *dress*, and one that would make Lanvin-Castillo think twice.

Are we still friends?

Little Cinema Movie Theater
Dear Sirs:

I called your theater yesterday afternoon and I said to the woman who answered the phone, "Young lady, will you please tell me at what time this evening you are showing *La Strada?* Also, please tell me at what time you are showing *Jailhouse Rock* with Elvis Presley." I was very calm. I didn't prejudice the case. Nor did I reveal by any variation in tone which picture I was trying to avoid. Anyway, she told me that *La Strada* began at 8:10 and *Jailhouse Rock* began at 10:16.

Not satisfied, I called in five minutes and in an assumed southern accent I asked the same question and got the same answer. It was, then, with complete confidence that my husband and I arrived at the theater at 8:10, to discover the opening credits of *Jailhouse Rock* coming on.

Now this may seem a very trifling mistake to you, but I assure you that my husband is a very nervous man (of course, he wasn't this nervous before *Jailhouse Rock*) and his condition has worsened noticeably. Little things, like the children's banging the basketball against the plate-glass doors, that he used to be able to pass off with a joke and a smile, now reduce him to screaming and shouting. This you must put on your conscience, Little Cinema.

You may ask why we didn't leave and come back for *La Strada*. Well, for one thing, we had already parked the car, and my husband didn't feel that at his age he could walk up and

248

down in front of the theater with that big bag of popcorn—and he wouldn't throw it away.

Aggrieved Moviegoer.

Dear Sister St. Joseph:

Colin tells me that he is playing the part of the Steering Wheel in the safety play. He feels, as I do, that he could bring a lot more to the part of the Stop Sign. I know Stop Sign is a speaking part, and while I realize that Colin is not ready for "leads," still he did memorize all three stanzas of *America, the Beautiful* and I myself would have absolute confidence in his ability to handle the line, "I am the stop sign. I am here to help you," which I understand constitutes the whole part.

Also, Colin is very tall for seven and I am sure we're agreed that height is very important for this particular role.

Finally let me mention (although I do not expect it to influence you) that I just happen to have a Stop-Sign costume, which I made for his brother three years ago.

Cordially, Colin's Mother.

Dear Doctor:

Those new sleeping pills you said would "fell an ox" don't work, either. Now what will I do?

Desperately, Jean.

I Have This Perfectly Marvelous Woman . . .

ๆๅ

BY JUNEIL PARMENTER

I was staring into my fifth cup of coffee, looking for eternal truth, I guess, or trying to figure out how to get the cleaning *and* washing *and* cooking done. *And* the ironing. And the petunias weeded. My little boy's record player was grinding out one of those jolly voices, "Make believe you're an engine, make believe you're an airplane. . . ." (Make believe you're anything except a little boy with a scratchy record player.) You know the sort.

Anyway, suddenly it seemed like a good idea. I'll make believe I'm a cleaning woman. I'm this perfectly marvelous cleaning woman and I'll clean house. For some reason it has always been easier for me to straighten up somebody else's house. While she's off in another room minding her baby, it is easy to pick up his toys. Or if your neighbor is sick, it's no great effort to mop her floors.

On the other hand, if you pick up your own baby's toys you really ought to sort them, or boil them, and there's no end to it. Or if you dust your own piano, you wonder if maybe you shouldn't refinish it, or roll it out and look for the things that get lost under pianos.

So I made believe I'm this perfectly marvelous cleaning woman. My name was Annette and I was great and strong and intelligent. The first thing I did was clean off the empty coffee cups. Then I made the beds, did the dishes, wiped the floors, dusted the living room. I was a wonder! By then it was eleven o'clock. So the lady of the house fixed a big lunch and then Annette ran the vacuum and hung out the wash. The phone rang and it was one of those bright cheerful voices that either want to sell you something or want you to collect funds for the benefit of some disease they haven't even discovered yet. So, Annette said that I, Mrs. Parmenter, was out and wouldn't be back till suppertime.

In the rest of that week Annette got rid of three awning salesmen on the phone and one very good friend whose voice she didn't recognize soon enough, but who recognized Annette's voice.

Annette worked like a charm for a whole week, from nine till four. Too hard, really. Annette is too conscientious. The evil day came when Annette quit. She said she was never coming back. She said some people leave their shoes right in the living room and there's a turtle on the back porch. Also she was out of laundry soap and her legs hurt.

That night we had canned beans and Spam for supper.

"Isn't Annette *ever* coming back?" the kids asked wistfully.

"No," I said. "She's gone to work on a wiring bank at an electronics factory out of town."

"Couldn't we get another one?" they asked. "She could be named Flora and she could be a good cook."

"Flora has varicose veins and a bad disposition. Also, she borrows money."

"Huldah?" my daughter suggested. Hmm, well, maybe. Huldah sort of appeals to me. That perfectly marvelous Swedish cooking and all. So next week Huldah goes to work. She is neat, strong, and intelligent and she doesn't mind about the turtle on the back porch. And after she quits, I can be Helen, and after she quits, I can be Lois. There's no end to it! The more I realize how it could never end, I think I, and by *I* I mean Annette, Huldah, Helen, and Lois, I think we will all get a job in an electronics plant out of town.

There Was a Pope
Named John

꧁

BY XAVIER RYNNE

Pope John XXIII died on June 3, 1963, at 7:49 A.M. Few pontiffs labored as hard as John for unity among Christians. None succeeded so completely in convincing the world of his sincerity. Non-Catholics and non-Christians turned to him as to a father.

Angelo Roncalli did what he said the council would do: he opened the windows of the Church and let in fresh air. He died at eighty-one; yet he was a man of today. The word *aggiornamento*, with which his reign will always be associated, is based on the word for *today* in Italian and means a "bringing up to date."

In his last illness he said to his physician, "Don't look so worried. My bags are packed and I'm ready to go." His humility had a rare quality. He wrote in his diary, August 12, 1961: "The Vicar of Christ? Ah, I am not worthy of this title—I, the poor son of Battista and Maria Anna Roncalli, two good Christians, to be sure, but so modest and so humble!"

A 1929 entry, on the occasion of his twenty-fifth anniversary as a priest, is unforgettable: "Countless priests already dead or still living after twenty-five years of priesthood have accomplished wonders in the apostolate and the sanctification of souls. And I, what have I done? My Jesus, mercy! But while I humble myself for the little or nothing I have achieved up to now, I raise my eyes toward the future. There still remains light in front of me; there still remains the hope of doing some good. Therefore, I take up my staff again, which from now on will be the staff of old age, and I go forward to meet whatever the Lord wishes for me."

His three most considerable claims on history's attention are his convocation of the first council of the Church to be held in a hundred years and his authorship of two great encyclicals: *Mater et Magistra*, which brought up to date the social teaching of Leo XIII's *Rerum Novarum*, and *Pacem in Terris*, the first encyclical ever addressed not only to the Catholic clergy and laity but to "all men of goodwill."

In some respects Pope John was quite old-fashioned. He wore the *camauro*, or fur-trimmed cap, associated with Renaissance rather than modern Popes. His homilies at St. Peter's were exactly what he might have said if he had been a small-town pastor. He also said his prayers as if he were on familiar terms with angels and saints.

These very old-fashioned qualities disarmed his critics in the Vatican entourage. They could not understand how a man of such spiritual simplicity could be revolutionary in his approach to age-old Catholic usages. They missed the point that as he saw it the mission of the papacy was twofold. "Our sacred obligation is not only to take care of this precious treasure (the deposit of faith) as if we had only to worry about the past," he said in 1962. "We must also devote ourselves, with joy and without fear, to the work of giving this ancient and eternal doctrine a relevancy corresponding to the conditions of our era." Prelates who fear change ("Fear," Pope John said, "comes only from a lack of faith") and resist it with denunciations and condemnations, subscribe to the first half only; those who see progress in change alone tend to think exclusively of the latter half. Pope John believed in both and acted on both.

In 1954 he introduced himself to his new parishioners of Venice. "I wish to speak to you with the utmost frankness. You have waited impatiently for me; people have told you about me and have written accounts that far surpass my merits. I introduce myself as I really am. Like every other person who lives here on earth, I come from a definite family and place. Thank God, I enjoy bodily health and a little good sense, which allows me to see matters quickly and clearly. Ever ready to love people, I stand by the law of the Gospel, a respecter of my own rights and of those of others, a fact which prevents me from doing harm to anybody and which encourages me to do good to all.

"I come of humble stock. I was raised in the kind of poverty which is confining but beneficial, which demands little, but which guarantees the development of the noblest and greatest virtues and which prepares one for the steep ascent of the mountain of life. Providence drew me out of my native village and made me traverse the roads of the world in the East and in the West.

"The same Providence made me embrace men who were different both by religion and by ideology. God made me face acute and threatening social problems, in the presence of which I kept a calm and balanced judgment and imagination in order to evaluate matters accurately, ever preoccupied, out of my respect for Catholic doctrinal and moral principles, not with what separates people and provokes conflicts, but rather with what unites men."

The Venetians loved their new pastor, who instead of condemning the annual Venice Film Festival, as his predecessors had done, gave it his blessing and acted as host to its committees and participants.

On his election as Pope in 1958 he chose a name unused for centuries. "Nearly all (the pontiffs named John) had a brief pontificate," he said to the cardinals, indicating that he knew full well why some of the electors might have chosen him. In his diary he confessed, in his simple and direct manner, "In the first days of my pontifical service I did not fully realize what it meant to be Bishop of Rome and therefore the pastor of the universal Church. Then, one week after another, full light spread and I felt at home, as if I had not done anything else all my life."

The pontificate of John XXIII was brief, four and a half years, the shortest since that of Pius VIII (1829–30), but no pontificate in our century has had vaster implications for the future.

Cardinal Suenens, during Second Vatican's second-session period of crisis, reminded his hearers of the world's feelings toward Pope John. "The television, the radio, and the press brought his death so close to us that it was like a death in the family. Never has the whole world taken part at such close quarters in the poignant stages of a mortal sickness. The death of John XXIII was precious in the sight of the world.

"At Castel Gandolfo in July, 1962, John the twenty-third had spent a day, pen in hand, studying the preparatory schemata. In the course of an audience he read aloud some of the notes he had written in the margin. Then suddenly he stopped and said, 'Oh, I know what my personal part in the preparation of the council will be.' And after a pause he concluded, 'It will be suffering.'

"John the twenty-third was the Pope of dialogue and this has special reference to the men of our time.

"It is not easy to make the world of today hear the voice of the Church. It is drowned by too much noise; there is too much static and interference in the air for the message to get through.

"In spite of these obstacles John the twenty-third managed to make himself heard: he broke through the sound barrier.

"John awakened a response.

"Men recognized his voice, a voice speaking to them of God, but also of human brotherhood, of the reestablishment of social justice, of a peace to be established throughout the whole world.

"This is why they wept for him as children for their father, pressing around him to receive his blessing. The poor wept for him; they knew he was one of them and that he was dying poor like them, thanking God for the poverty that for him had been such a grace. The prisoners wept for him: he had visited them and encouraged them with his presence. Who does not remember that visit to the prison of Rome? Among the prisoners were two murderers. After having heard the Holy Father, one of them approached and said, 'These words of hope that you have just spoken, do they also apply to me, such a great sinner?'

"The Pope's answer was to open his arms and clasp him to his heart.

"This prisoner is surely a symbol of mankind, close to the heart of John the twenty-third."

TAKE-HOME PAY

The payroll of a certain large corporation is made out every week by an "electronic brain." Once, through error, the machine issued a check to one production worker for $00.00.

The astonished man stared at it for several minutes, then moaned, "I've always been afraid that this would happen some-day. My deductions have at last caught up with my salary!"

Wall Street Journal.

DIAGNOSIS

During the recent recession a manufacturing firm hired an efficiency expert to search out possible economies. His presence irked some of the long-time employees.

The expert approached one veteran clerk. "What, exactly, do you do here?" he asked.

"Not a thing," replied the man with a smirk.

The expert made a note on the pad and moved on to the next desk. Here, too, the answer was a surly "Nothing!"

"Ah-ha," murmured the expert sagely and noted on his pad: "Duplication."

American Weekly.

THE MASTER TOUCH

The hour was late and the lone bus passenger was annoyed when a decidedly intoxicated man got on and slumped into the seat beside him. His misgivings increased when the other turned to him and said thickly, "Got any money?"

"No," the man replied shortly to head off an impending "touch."

The drunk gave him a long look, then leaned forward and spoke impressively. "I should try to get some if I were you," he said. "You would find it very useful."

Quote.

RAIN IN SUMMER

Summer rain is like catsup in a bottle: you become exasperated because you don't get any, then suddenly you get too much.

Brock Bell in Household.

ARTIST'S LONG

Fernandel, the French comedian, was trying out a new barber-shop. The barber, overjoyed at having such a celebrity in his chair, was extremely anxious to please. When he finished he held a mirror in back of Fernandel's head and asked anxiously, "Is that all right?"

Fernandel flashed the famous smile. "Almost. Just a little longer in the back, please," he said.

Journal of the American Medical Association.

RUSES OF ADVERSITY

A Czechoslovakian patriot had to depart hurriedly via the fire escape when the secret police came knocking at the door. He raced down back alleys until he came to a small café where he was well known.

"I know it's late," he said to the astonished proprietor, "but do you suppose you could cache a small Czech?"

Coronet.

SICKLY PIETY

If you can't joke about your religion, you're not steadfast in your piety—you're simply afflicted with the disease of "religiosity."

Sydney J. Harris.

TRADE NOT AID

Casey Stengel, when manager of the New York Yankees, was a great one for masking his wisdom with wit. Said he, "Never trade a player because he's a drunk. Chances are he'll get so sore

259

at you he'll give up drinking, and then every time you play against him, he'll murder you."

Joe McCarthy in the American Weekly.

MAN WITH A HOE

Four golfers were on the green when a ball rolled onto it. One of them winked at the others and putted the ball into the hole. A few seconds later a fat fellow came puffing up. "Did any of you see a ball around here?" he asked.

"Yeah," one golfer replied. "It's in the hole."

The fat man waddled over to the cup, stared unbelievingly down at the ball, and then picked it out of the cup. Then he ran down the fairway shouting, "Hey, Louie! I got a nine!"

Minneapolis Star.

URBAN RENEWAL

During the last days of the Christmas rush a frenzied clerk, overwhelmed by the last-minute shoppers, was making out a sales slip. As the customer gave her name and address, the clerk, surveying the maze of confusion about her, remarked, "It's a madhouse, isn't it?"

"No," the customer replied frostily. "It's a private residence."

Lucille Goodyear.

CONFUSION OF TONGUES

The personnel manager of the department store asked the job-seeking young man what he had been doing for the past few years.

"I was in Yale," the applicant said.

"Well, well," said the personnel manager, deeply impressed.

"I'll put you in charge of counting cash in the auditor's office."

A few days later, making his rounds, the personnel manager watched the newcomer stacking up bills and coins. He stopped by and said to him, "By the way, what did you say your name was?"

"Yim Yackson," the young man replied.

Joe McCarthy in the American Weekly.

INSOMNIA???

A hillbilly was undergoing a physical examination. "Have you been sleeping well lately?" the doctor inquired.

The mountaineer thought a moment, then drawled, "I sleep real good nights, and purty good mornings. But afternoons," he complained, "I jest toss and turn."

Woodmen of the World.

THE GENIUS IN US

A factory manager's assistant, being a bright young man, was selected by "the boys" to buy a wedding gift for the boss.

So the assistant visited all the two thousand employees and collected a quarter from each. With the $500 he bought two thousand packs of cigarettes, the kind with a gift coupon inside the pack.

He traded the coupons in for a silver coffee service and gave that to the boss as a wedding gift. Then he gave each employee a pack of cigarettes.

When the firm's president heard about this goings on, he was so intrigued by the young man's ingenuity that he ordered him to report at once. "I can use a man like him in management," he explained.

But he had to wait two weeks before the interview could take place. With the five thousand trading stamps the ingenious one had collected when he bought the cigarettes, he got himself a complete fishing outfit and left on vacation.

Sam Pavlovic in the St. Paul Pioneer Press.

VOTE OF CONFIDENCE

A man handed a $1 bill to a post-office clerk to pay for 34¢ postage due on a parcel. The clerk searched his change drawer, found that he didn't have any pennies, and asked the man if he couldn't produce 4¢ more to make the exchange come out even.

The customer then searched *his* pockets and discovered that he, too, had no pennies. In his wallet, however, he found a 4¢ stamp and he offered this to the clerk.

"I'm sorry, sir," the clerk pointed out with dignity. "The post office cannot accept stamps."

Maclean's.

THE GROVES OF ACADEME

At a class reunion the wealthiest person attending was also the one who had been the lowest ranking student. The "brains" of the class couldn't understand how anyone so dumb could amass such a fortune while they still struggled along, trying to make ends meet.

"Tell us," one asked, "what was the secret of your success?"

The rich classmate blinked in surprise. "Why, the answer is very simple. I own a department store. I buy a dress for one dollar, for example, and sell it for four dollars. That way I always make my three percent."

S. J. Gudge.

RUSES OF ADVERSITY

On a recent trip to Key West, Florida, my husband and I were fishing in a small motorboat when we were caught in a sudden downpour. We became frightened at the change in weather but were relieved when the Coast Guard picked us up.

Back at their headquarters we found ourselves mightily shaken up, wet, and embarrassed at our situation. However, the tension was broken when we overheard the radioman reporting in. "Nobody hurt, sir. We just have a couple of Damp Yankees here."

Mrs. Deane Binder.

ONLY IN AMERICA

The lady ahead of me in the supermarket checkout line patiently waited while the clerk rang up her purchases. Of items priced at three for 41¢ she bought two; of those at five for 43¢, she bought four; of others at three for 23¢, she bought two.

Noting the smile on my face, she explained, "No store is going to tell *me* how many of what to buy!"

Mrs. S. Lee.

THE MODERN TOAST

Overheard in a Washington, D.C., bar: "Well, here's to your Health, Education, and Welfare!"

Washington Daily News.

CABALA

A New York cab driver, carrying a nun as a passenger, went through a red light and was immediately stopped by a policeman. The officer noted the Sister in the cab and, after writing the ticket, tipped his cap and drove off.

"Well, at last I've seen the day!" exclaimed a bystander. "The cabbie goes through a red light and the cop tips his hat to him!"

Philadelphia Inquirer.

On a recent trip to New York City I hailed a cab on Broadway and asked the driver to take me to Penn Station. He expertly wove through traffic, missing parked cars and pedestrians by inches. I felt a great sense of security in riding with such an expert. My faith was shattered, however, when we pulled up to the station. He peered nearsightedly at the meter and after several false attempts whipped out a thick reading glass to discover the amount.

Mrs. S. Lee.

COLOR LINE

Every man is said to show up sometimes in his "true colors." But what are they? When a man is rebellious, he is red; when he is cowardly, yellow; when he is honest, white; when he is loyal, blue; when he is inexperienced, green. But when he is only boring he is colorless.

Catholic Living.

RUSES OF ADVERSITY

A soldier at Fort Baker, California, who was working as personnel clerk received a document in his morning mail. It was not addressed to him, so he initialed it and passed it on to the officer for whom it was intended.

He promptly got it back with this note attached: "This document did not concern you. Please erase your initials and initial your erasure."

San Francisco Examiner.

LET THERE BE LIGHT

A Chinese scholar was lecturing at Columbia University when all the lights in the auditorium suddenly went out. Unperturbed, the lecturer asked all members of the audience to raise their hands. They did and the lights immediately came on again.

"Proves wisdom of old Chinese saying," the scholar remarked with satisfaction. "Many hands make light work."

Saturday Review.

WHAT'S UP?

Two dear old ladies were taking advantage of ladies' day at the local ball park. Said one to the other, "Is measles catching?"

"I think so," replied the other. "What I want to know is, who is pitching?"

Harry Donen.

VIVACIOUS LADIES

A lady went into the St. Cloud, Minnesota, police station to pay a small traffic fine. While she was fumbling through her purse for money, she dropped some green trading stamps on the floor.

The desk sergeant noticed the stamps drop and, being a gentleman, he stooped, picked up the stamps, and said, "Here, lady. Here are your green stamps."

The lady beamed with joy. "Why, do you give green stamps, too?" she asked ecstatically. "I must come here more often!"

Paul Light in the St. Paul Pioneer Press.

DAYS IN COURT

A lawyer was browbeating a witness. "I understand," he snarled, "that you called on the defendant. What did he say to you at that time?"

Counsel for the other side objected that an answer would be hearsay and not admissible. The first lawyer contended that direct testimony as to what was said did not constitute hearsay. A long argument followed. The judge retired to chambers to consider the point. He returned after some time to rule that the question was a proper one.

"Now," continued the lawyer triumphantly, "what did the defendant tell you when you called on him?"

"I don't know. He wasn't home, sir," was the meek reply.

Rays of Sunshine.

EMPLOYMENT OPPORTUNITIES

Called up by his draft board and asked his occupation a young man answered, "I'm a comedian."

"That so?" mocked his examiner. "Let's see you do something funny."

So the city lad turned to the long line of men waiting their turns behind him and called out, "You can go home, fellows. I got the job!"

Mrs. Louis Binder.

PRESCRIPTION

A tough, loudmouthed man appeared at his doctor's office demanding immediate attention.

"Well, well, Mr. Hornblow," said the doctor. "Is this an emergency?"

"It sure is," croaked the man, pointing to his throat. "Hear that? Every time I try to talk all that comes out is a whisper."

"It's nothing serious. Just a mild laryngitis."

"What can I do for it?" insisted the man.

"Listen," the doctor answered.

Journal of American Medical Association.

BOOTLESS CURE

A sailor limped into a naval hospital to have his foot X-rayed and was asked to wait for the results. Some time later an orderly appeared and handed the sailor a large pill.

Just then a mother with a small child in need of immediate attention entered. After the orderly disappeared with the new patient, the sailor hobbled over to get a glass of water, swallowed the pill, and sat down to wait.

Some time later the orderly reappeared carrying a bucket of water. "OK," he said, "let's drop the pill in this bucket and soak the foot."

Quote.

WHERE THERE'S SMOKE

A man in the mountains of Arizona came upon an Indian who was sending up smoke signals. When asked how big a fire he usually built, the Indian replied, "It all depends. You see, I have to know whether it's a local or a long-distance call."

C. Kennedy.

SOUND OF MUSIC

A man recently came up to the gifted pianist George Shearing and asked him whether he had been blind all his life.

"No," said the forty-five-year-old Shearing. "Not yet."

Morris Bender.

THE PLOT QUICKENS

When Doubleday's publicity man began mulling over the publishing firm's novel *It Can't Always Be Caviar*, a spy story

267

incorporating recipes for delectable food, he hit upon the idea of soliciting dishes appropriate for spy stories from the editorial staff. Among the offered delicacies were: Cop Suey, Murderer's Roe, Borscht Karloff, Thicken Plot Pie, Just Desserts, Who-Do-Nuts, Double Cross Buns, Cole Slaughter.

Saturday Review.

AN ECUMENICAL PARKING LOT

The spirit of ecumenism seems to have spread everywhere. A sign on the parking lot of a Catholic church in Detroit says: "Please Face All Cars East."

Mitch Pieronek.

SIGNS OF THE TIMES

In the window of a maternity-garment shop: "Clothes to make your heir less apparent."

Good Housekeeping.

CANNIBALS AND WINGS

A Hollywood producer relates how one African headhunter explained his first glimpse of a TV set to another. "It's a wonderful machine where they shrink the whole body."

Hollywood Reporter.

POPE JOHN'S SECRET SEMINARY

I first met Pope John, then Archbishop Roncalli, in September, 1945. He was apostolic nuncio to France and I was director of the Catholic Relief Services.

268

I had received a surprising call from the archbishop. Would I come to see him right away? I hurried to his small bedroom-office. One other man was in the room: Msgr. Egidio Vagnozzi, now an archbishop, and apostolic delegate to the United States. Archbishop Roncalli let him do the talking.

"The archbishop has established a seminary at the prisoner-of-war camp at Chartres. It admits Germans who had been studying for the priesthood before the war, or who might wish to begin now." Monsignor Vagnozzi paused, then added carefully, "The French Government knows nothing of its existence."

I gasped. The plan was audacious. The communists were strong in both Cabinet and National Assembly. Here was something the communists would never understand—an act of Christian forgiveness toward the Germans on the part of France. Hitler's persecutions had thinned the ranks of the Catholic clergy. Archbishop Roncalli's secret seminary would create a cadre of priests who would work for the moral reconstruction of their country.

"At present," Monsignor Vagnozzi went on, "five hundred and sixty-two German prisoners are enrolled in the seminary. But we are in trouble. Our seminarians are too weak to study. They cannot carry on their rigorous studies on prisoners' rations."

I had food: three million pounds of it. And I had trucks to convoy it to Chartres. But food for Germans, when many Frenchmen were still hungry? The project must indeed be kept secret from both government and public.

Twice a week for a full year four trucks, driven by American GI's who had volunteered for the job, took food to the secret seminary at Chartres under cover of night. No one ever found out.

In May, 1946, I was present when Archbishop Roncalli ordained the first two prisoners-of-war. The principal speaker was a four-star French general. A German sergeant translated his words. "Western Europe must unite to survive," the general said. "There must never be another war between us. You men are going home to tie a bond between France and Germany through the unity of Christ."

I glanced at Cardinal Roncalli. His smile was a mile wide.

ECUMENISM IN NORTHERN IRELAND

A recent visitor to Belfast, capital of Northern Ireland, has reported a softening of its traditional anti-Catholicism. On a wall he found this slogan scrawled: "Down with all Popes except Pope John."

America.

MEANS TO END

Hugh Burnett, television producer for the British Broadcasting Corp., decided he needed some professional help in preparing two satirical programs, one on heaven and the other on hell. He wrote to Father Agnellus Andrew, O.F.M., BBC's Catholic consultant, asking how he could get the official Roman Catholic view of heaven and hell. The memorandum he got back was in one word: *Die*.

NCWC.

FLIGHTS OF FANCY

Peopled: Words bounced off as though they were wearing thought-proof vests.—*Walter Farrell, O.P.*
Money is lost in more ways than won.—*Louise Vesci.*
Jaywalkers adagioing across the street—*Morris Bender.*

The women kept up a purring acquaintance.—*Harold Helfer.*
The wheels of the train were square and the tracks had hiccups.
   —*C. W. Grafton.*
Flag snapping to attention—*Robert Brault.*
Watching for a parking place to pass by—*Clare Marie Garden.*